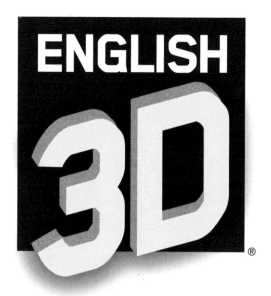

ENGLISH 3D®

ISSUES

COURSE II

Credits and acknowledgments appear on pages 206–208, which constitute an extension of this copyright page.

Copyright © 2014 by Scholastic Inc.

All rights reserved.   Published by Scholastic Inc.   Printed in the U.S.A.

ISBN-13: 978-0-545-62973-7

ISBN-10: 0-545-62973-X

SCHOLASTIC, ENGLISH 3D, and associated logos are trademarks and/or registered trademarks of Scholastic Inc.

Other company names, brand names, and product names are the property and/or trademarks of their respective owners. Scholastic does not endorse any product or business entity mentioned herein.

Scholastic is constantly working to lessen the environmental impact of our manufacturing processes.

To view our industry-leading paper procurement policy, visit www.scholastic.com/paperpolicy.

1 2 3 4 5 6 7 8 9 10   23   22 21 20 19 18 17 16 15 14 13

 Text pages printed on 10% PCW recycled paper.

TABLE OF **CONTENTS**

Academic Words in *Issues* Texts

Words to Go: High-utility words that you will encounter in other texts and content areas are **highlighted in yellow**.

Words to Know: Topic-related words that you can use to discuss and write about the Issue are **boldface**.

TEEN SLEEP Can teens be trusted to know
their limit when it comes to credit?
READY TO WORK TEENS & MONEY
Table of Contents **3**

DO TEENS NEED A WAKE-UP CALL WHEN IT COMES TO SLEEP?

Data File

Briiiiiiiing! It's time to wake up and learn the truth about sleep: it's vital to our health and well-being. Are you getting enough?

Survey Says

- A poll of 1,602 teenagers across the United States found that teens get an average of about seven and a half hours of sleep on school nights.
- Teens sleep less as they get older. In 8th grade, they average 8.1 hours of sleep. By 12th grade, the average drops to 6.9 hours.
- Only 20% of teens are getting the optimal amount of sleep—9 hours or more.

(Source: National Sleep Foundation, 2006)

Is Technology Taking a Toll?

- 72% of 13- to 18-year-olds questioned bring their cell phones into their bedrooms and use them when they are trying to go to sleep.
- 56% of **adolescents** text in the hour before trying to go to sleep every night or almost every night.
- 77% of 13- to 18-year-olds use a computer in the hour before going to bed.
- 50% of teens watch TV within one hour of trying to go to sleep.

(Source: National Sleep Foundation, 2011)

Making It Legal

In 2009, California State Representative Zoe Lofgren cosponsored a bill in Congress called the Zzz's to A's Resolution, which proposed that secondary schools should begin the school day no earlier than 9:00 in the morning. The resolution was not enacted.

(Source: opencongress.org, 2009)

WHO NEEDS SLEEP?

Maybe you do. Here's what you need to know about slumber, from A to Zzzzzz's.

by Kirsten Weir

Quick quiz: How much of your life will you spend sleeping? Answer: A whopping one-third. For something we spend so much time doing, we don't often give slumber the credit—or attention—it deserves. A study by the National Sleep Foundation (NSF) found that 60 percent of middle and high school students felt tired during the day, and 15 percent had fallen asleep in school during the last year. "I'm definitely tired during the week," says Leah Schaffer, a 17-year-old junior from Oxford, Michigan. "I nod off a lot in chemistry." But why is sleep so important? And why are so few of us getting enough?

SLEEPLESSNESS KILLS

When we sleep, we cycle through five well-defined **stages**. Between **stages** 1 and 4, we sink deeper and deeper into sleep. Heart rate and body temperature drop. Brain waves slow down and muscles relax completely.

Fifteen percent of teens say they have fallen asleep in school in the past year.

Then we enter the fifth **stage** of sleep: rapid eye movement, or REM, sleep. During this **stage**, our eyes dart back and forth below the eyelids, and our brain waves speed up again to the same levels as when we're awake. Most dreaming occurs during REM sleep. People need both non-REM and REM sleep in order to get a good night's rest. During a full night of sleep, we cycle through all five sleep **stages** between three and five times.

Scientists know that we have to sleep. Repeated experiments with lab rats have shown that rats will die from lack of sleep long before they die from lack of food. **Sleep-deprived** people, however, don't drop dead, but they do suffer health problems. Humans who go days without sleep begin to have digestive troubles, such as diarrhea and stomach pain. They experience memory problems and hallucinations and can quickly become paranoid.

However, scientists still aren't certain why we need to snooze. One theory is that while we sleep, our bodies repair muscles and other tissues. Some researchers believe that sleeping and dreaming are necessary for the

The Stages of Sleep

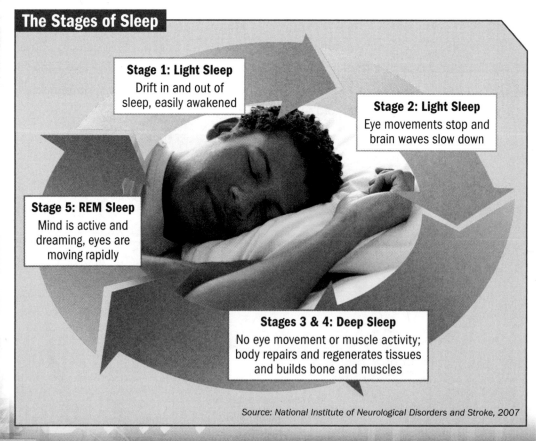

Stage 1: Light Sleep
Drift in and out of sleep, easily awakened

Stage 2: Light Sleep
Eye movements stop and brain waves slow down

Stage 5: REM Sleep
Mind is active and dreaming, eyes are moving rapidly

Stages 3 & 4: Deep Sleep
No eye movement or muscle activity; body repairs and regenerates tissues and builds bone and muscles

Source: National Institute of Neurological Disorders and Stroke, 2007

brain to organize and store memories. Others think we slow down at night to conserve energy.

Some researchers believe that sleeping and dreaming are necessary for the brain to organize and store memories.

SETTING YOUR BODY CLOCK

Adults need about eight hours of sleep each night, but young people need even more. "Kids from about 10 to 18 need a little more than nine hours of sleep a night, on average," says Dr. Mary Carskadon, a sleep researcher and member of the NSF task force on sleep and teens. Yet Carskadon has found that most teens sleep an average of seven hours a night.

Busy schedules are only part of the problem. During **adolescence**, the body's internal clock gets pushed back so that a person doesn't feel sleepy until later in the evening. The result? Teens want to stay up later at night and sleep later in the morning. "I **tend to** be tired in the morning, and toward the end of the day I wake up," Leah says. To make matters worse, nighttime habits can also **affect** the body's clock. One way the body learns when to sleep is through light cues. Staying up late in a bright room or staring at a brightly lit TV or computer screen can push the internal clock back even later.

SICK AND TIRED

The short-term effects of too little sleep are obvious enough. Too little shut-eye can leave you feeling fuzzy-headed and unable to concentrate. "Almost all teenagers, as they reach **puberty**, become walking zombies because they are getting far too little sleep," says Cornell University psychologist James Maas in the American Psychological Association's *Monitor on Psychology*. Over time, skimping on sleep can cause a sleep debt to accumulate, and that can have serious **consequences**. "As the sleep **deficit** goes on week after week, your body changes," Carskadon adds.

Sleep-deprived people have problems with learning and memory. Mood is also **affected**, and overtired teens can show mood problems that mimic depression. In some cases, youths may be prescribed medication for depression when, in fact, they're just way behind on sleep. Also, the **hormone** cortisol, which is associated with stress, can build up in the **sleep-deprived**. High cortisol levels weaken the immune system, making a person more susceptible to illness.

New studies are also revealing that sleep debt can mess with **metabolism**, the chemical processes that occur within an organism to sustain life. "If you aren't getting enough sleep, you're likely to eat more and also process food differently," Carskadon reports. Those metabolic changes can lead to weight gain and related health problems, including diabetes.

Unfortunately, sleep debt is hard to overcome. Sleeping in on weekends is your body's way of playing catch-up—but if you overdo it, you could be making matters worse. Carskadon suggests sleeping for an extra hour or two, but not all day. Your body will thank you for it Monday morning, she says.

Still, it's important to listen to your body and give it the rest it craves. "Kids need to be happier," says Carskadon. "I think if they had more sleep, they'd be happier."

Secrets of the Sandman

Insomnia occurs when a person can't fall asleep or awakens too early. If you have trouble sleeping on a regular basis, these tips could help you get some shut-eye:

1 Keep your bedroom dark at night and bright in the morning, since light cues help set your body's internal clock.

2 Exercise during the day, no fewer than three hours before bedtime.

3 Avoid big meals at night; eat dinner at least two hours before going to bed.

4 Go to bed at the same time every night to train your body when to sleep.

5 Are you staring at the clock and worrying that you aren't getting a good night's sleep? Turn the clock toward the wall and relax.

6 If you can't fall asleep, get out of bed. Teach your body that your bed is for sleeping.

7 Think positive thoughts. Instead of thinking "I'm going to be so tired tomorrow," try telling yourself "I'm probably getting more rest than I realize."

8 Don't drink caffeine after lunchtime.

9 Don't sleep in all day on weekends—it will confuse your body's clock. If you feel you need to catch up on sleep, take a 30- to 40-minute nap during the day.

10 Have a relaxing bedtime routine.

SLEEP IS ONE THING MISSING IN BUSY TEENAGE LIVES

by Denise Grady

At 6:30 in the morning, a strapping teenager on the cusp of manhood can look an awful lot like a newborn puppy, with eyes that won't open and a powerful instinct to curl up under something warm.

Is this the same person who swore he wasn't tired at 10:30 the night before while he traded instant messages with six different friends at once, and who will probably do it again tonight?

Parents know the **adolescent** drill all too well: stay up past 11 or 12 on school nights, stagger out of bed at 6 or 7, shower interminably, eat a token breakfast, and bolt. Yawn through school, perk up for sports or clubs, fight sleep while doing homework. Come to life at 9 p.m., deny fatigue and stay up well after parents have collapsed into bed. Holidays and weekends, stay up half the night and then "binge sleep" until noon or beyond. Sunday night, restart the cycle of late to bed and early to rise.

1 Americans are said to be a **sleep-deprived** people, and teenagers are the worst of the lot. Most are lucky to get six, seven, or eight hours of sleep a night, even though studies have shown repeatedly that people in their teens and possibly even early 20s need nine to 10 hours. Many live in a state of chronic sleep **deficit** that can **affect** mood, behavior, schoolwork, and reaction time.

> **Americans are said to be a sleep-deprived people, and teenagers are the worst of the lot.**

Dr. Mary Carskadon, a sleep researcher at Brown University, describes **sleep-deprived** teenagers as existing in a "kind of gray cloud."

"We just ignore these bad feelings from not enough sleep and get used to it," she said. "We forget what it's like to feel good, and how much more efficiently you can do things." Physical, emotional, and social **factors** seem to conspire against letting **adolescents** get enough sleep.

When teenagers insist that they are not tired at 9 or 10 p.m., they are very likely telling the truth. For reasons that are not fully understood, Dr. Carskadon said, their body clocks shift, so that their natural **tendency** is to stay up later at night and wake up later in the morning than when they were younger. But that inner clock often clashes with the outer world:

early starting times in high school and demanding schedules of sports, clubs, music lessons, homework, and part-time jobs.

There are **consequences**. For one thing, lack of sleep can interfere with learning: tired students have a hard time paying attention, and even if they do somehow manage to focus, they may forget what they were taught because memory formation takes place partly during sleep.

In *Adolescent Sleep Patterns*, a book published in August and edited by Dr. Carskadon, she wrote, "The students may be in school, but their brains are at home on their pillows."

Consequences of Sleep Deprivation

BEHAVIORAL

Brain
- Depressed mood—symptoms include feeling stressed, angry, or sad
- Trouble remembering new information and making memories
- Difficulty paying attention and learning
- Increased aggressive or violent behavior

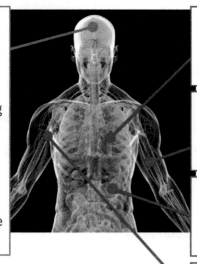

PHYSICAL

Heart
- Changes in heart rate
- Increased risk of heart disease, heart attacks, or strokes

Muscles
- Slower reaction times and impaired coordination
- Feeling shaky, weak, or achy

Pancreas
- Increased risk of Type 2 diabetes
- Increased risk of obesity due to slower metabolism

Immune System
- Increased chances of illness

Source: Maas & Robbins, 2011.

Tired teenagers can be as cranky as tired two-year-olds, and even less fun to deal with. More seriously, **sleep deprivation** can bring on feelings of stress, anger, and sadness.

> **Sleep deprivation can bring on feelings of stress, anger, and sadness.**

Dr. Carskadon said studies had repeatedly linked **sleep deprivation** to depressed mood—a temporary case of the blues, not the same as clinical depression.

"In every study where we've looked at it, it's crystal clear that kids who sleep less report more depressed mood," she said.

In one experiment, Dr. Carskadon said, teenagers were shown various photographs, and a researcher gauged their emotional reactions.

"Kids not getting enough sleep are less likely to **respond** in a positive way to positive things in the environment, and more likely to **respond** in a negative way to negative things," she said.

Pictures that most people would enjoy—images of cute babies, or of swimmers playing in waterfalls in Hawaii—do nothing for tired teenagers. "They're flat in their **response**," Dr. Carskadon said. "They don't say they felt pleasure. But if they see something negative, like a pizza with a big roach on it or a picture of the most disgusting toilet, kids who are **sleep-deprived** sort of have a worse **response**. It makes them more angry than the kids who have had plenty of sleep. How does it translate into their real lives? We're not sure."

In her book, Dr. Carskadon noted that studies in animals showed that sleep loss was associated with "marked increases in aggressive behavior and violence."

Lack of sleep may take its toll physically as well. Growth **hormone** and sex **hormones** are secreted during sleep, but it is not known whether missing out on sleep disrupts **hormonal** patterns. Studies have shown that **sleep deprivation** may also diminish the body's ability to process glucose, and a prolonged sleep **deficit** can produce the kind of blood glucose levels found in people who are on the way to becoming diabetic.

DROWSY DRIVERS PULL OVER IF NECESSARY
FATIGUED ⊘ DRIVING

Drivers under 25 who are tired cause more than 50,000 accidents per year.

Studies in people and animals suggest that lack of sleep may also interfere with the working of the immune system and its ability to fight infections, but, Dr. Carskadon said, it is not clear whether sleep loss is linked to illness in people.

Lack of sleep also increases teenage drivers' already elevated risk of car accidents. According to the National Sleep Foundation, a nonprofit group, drowsiness or fatigue play a role in 100,000 traffic crashes a year, and drivers 25 or under cause more than half of those accidents. Sleep loss and drinking are an especially bad combination because fatigue greatly magnifies the effects of alcohol, according to a report by the sleep foundation.

❷ Many health experts and parents say that high school starting times—often before 8 a.m.—are largely to blame for students' perpetual exhaustion.

According to a poll in August by the sleep foundation, 80 percent of the people surveyed said high schools should not start before 8 a.m. The foundation favors 9 a.m.

Some school districts have already changed their schedules so that high school classes start later, between 8 and 9, instead of before 8. In some cases, the changes came about only after parents campaigned for them.

In Minnesota, the state medical association took a stand and wrote school superintendents a letter warning that early start times were incompatible with teenagers' body clocks, and bad for health, school performance, and driving. In 1996, Edina, Minnesota, a suburb of Minneapolis, changed its high school starting time from 7:25 to 8:30, and in 1997, Minneapolis changed high school opening times to 8:40 from 7:15.

Researchers from the University of Minnesota have been studying the changes and report that, for the most part, students and teachers prefer the later start times. Many parents now want middle school to start later as well. Teachers say students are less likely to fall asleep in morning classes, and some students say they get more sleep and are more likely to eat breakfast. Suburban schools say students behave better, and in the city schools, attendance and graduation rates have gone up and tardiness has decreased.

The drawbacks are that some students, especially in city schools, are unable to take part in after-school activities, and some say they are earning less at their after-school jobs.

But not all school districts are willing or able to alter their schedules because they do not have enough school buses to carry children from elementary, middle, and high school during the same hours. Some have concerns, too, that later schedules will interfere with after-school sports.

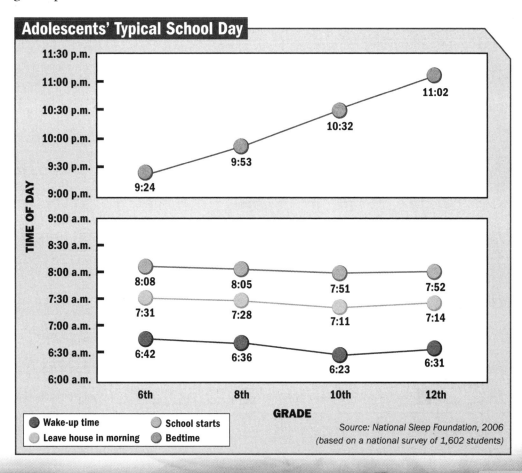

Adolescents' Typical School Day

TIME OF DAY

Bedtime line:
- 6th: 9:24
- 8th: 9:53
- 10th: 10:32
- 12th: 11:02

School starts line:
- 6th: 8:08
- 8th: 8:05
- 10th: 7:51
- 12th: 7:52

Leave house in morning line:
- 6th: 7:31
- 8th: 7:28
- 10th: 7:11
- 12th: 7:14

Wake-up time line:
- 6th: 6:42
- 8th: 6:36
- 10th: 6:23
- 12th: 6:31

GRADE: 6th, 8th, 10th, 12th

Legend:
- ● Wake-up time
- ● Leave house in morning
- ● School starts
- ● Bedtime

Source: National Sleep Foundation, 2006
(based on a national survey of 1,602 students)

According to the sleep foundation, individual schools and districts in 13 states have changed to later school start times. But many still start before 8 a.m., and nearly all before 9. A few schools are starting earlier.

❸ The military has shown more flexibility than some school districts. Concern about **sleep deprivation** led the United States Navy last April to change the "rack time," or sleeping hours, for young sailors—many of whom are in their late teens—at the Great Lakes base in Chicago, where all basic training is done.

Previously, the schedule allowed only six hours of sleep, from 10 p.m. until 4 a.m. The Navy first tried adding one hour by ordering lights out at 9 p.m., but psychologists who had studied sleep said that was the wrong **approach**.

"I toured the barracks after lights out, and found what we expected," said Dr. Jeff Dyche, a naval lieutenant and psychologist. "The recruits were lying in their racks staring at the ceiling. You can't force these kids to go to sleep that early."

Dr. Dyche said he and other psychologists briefed a three-star admiral about sleep research, especially Dr. Carskadon's work. The psychologists said young people could not fall asleep early and were at their sleepiest from 4 a.m. to 6 a.m. They recommended letting the recruits sleep later rather than ordering them to bed earlier, and allowing them eight hours of sleep a night.

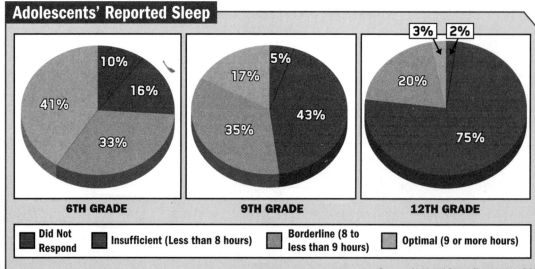

Adolescents' Reported Sleep

6TH GRADE: 10%, 16%, 41%, 33%

9TH GRADE: 5%, 17%, 43%, 35%

12TH GRADE: 3%, 2%, 20%, 75%

- Did Not Respond
- Insufficient (Less than 8 hours)
- Borderline (8 to less than 9 hours)
- Optimal (9 or more hours)

Source: National Sleep Foundation, 2006 (based on a national survey of 1,602 students)

The Navy changed its "rack time" from 10 p.m.–4 a.m. to 10 p.m.–6 a.m.

The admiral agreed, noting that his generation had slept eight hours during training. He made the rack time 10 p.m. to 6 a.m.

Navy researchers are studying the soldiers to see if the extra sleep makes a difference.

"They're looking at test scores, sleep patterns, sick call, and the number of times these kids get into trouble," Dr. Dyche said. "We want to compare it to years past and see what we get." Although the **data** are not in yet, he added, he expects "big dividends."

Doctors and sleep experts say parents need to play a stronger role in helping their teenagers to get more sleep.

Among the suggestions are setting a bedtime on school nights, being there to enforce it, and not letting the weekend hours drift so far out of line that they throw off the rest of the week.

Part of the strategy also includes limiting or banning television on school nights, as well as telephone and Internet socializing.

The intentions are noble, but perhaps not so easy to carry out, especially at 11:30 when the 15-year-old needs "just a few more minutes" to finish an English project or practice a solo for the next day's concert.

But it may be that a good night's sleep, given a chance, will sell itself. Dr. Carskadon said that one young man, who slept nine hours a night for a week as part of a study, told her: "You know, this is really good. I might try this even when the study's over."

UNDERSTANDING THE ZOMBIE TEEN'S BODY CLOCK

by Sue Shellenbarger

Many parents know the scene: The groggy, **sleep-deprived** teenager stumbles through breakfast and falls asleep over afternoon homework, only to spring to life, wide-eyed and alert, at 10 p.m.—just as Mom and Dad are nodding off.

Fortunately for parents, science has gotten more sophisticated at explaining why, starting at **puberty**, a teen's internal sleep-wake clock seems to go off the rails. Researchers are also connecting the dots between the resulting sleep loss and behavior long chalked up to just "being a teenager." This includes more risk-taking, less self-control, a drop in school performance, and a rise in the incidence of depression.

One 2010 study from the University of British Columbia, for example, found that sleep loss can hamper neuron growth in the brain during **adolescence**, a critical period for cognitive development.

Findings linking sleep loss to **adolescent** turbulence are "really revelatory," says Michael Terman, a professor of clinical psychology and psychiatry at Columbia University Medical Center and coauthor of *Chronotherapy*, a forthcoming book on resetting the body clock. "These are reactions to a basic change in the way teens' physiology and behavior is organized."

Despite such revelations, there are still no clear solutions for the teen-

The light from a bright computer screen can push a teen's body clock back even further.

zombie syndrome. Should a parent try to enforce strict wake-up and bedtimes, even though they conflict with the teen's body clock? Or try to create a workable sleep schedule around that natural cycle? Coupled with a **trend** toward predawn school start times and peer pressure to socialize online into the wee hours, the result can upset kids' health, school performance—and family peace.

Jeremy Kern, 16 years old, of San Diego, gets up at 6:30 a.m. for school and tries to fall asleep by 10 p.m. But a heavy load of homework and extracurricular activities, including playing saxophone in his school marching band and in a theater orchestra, often keeps him up later.

"I need 10 hours of sleep to not feel tired, and every single day I have to deal with being exhausted," Jeremy says. He stays awake during early-afternoon classes "by sheer force of will." And as research shows, sleep loss makes him more emotionally volatile, Jeremy says, like when he recently broke up with his girlfriend: "You are more irrational when you're **sleep deprived**. Your emotions are much harder to control."

Only 7.6 percent of teens get the recommended 9 to 10 hours of sleep, 23.5 percent get eight hours and 38.7 percent are seriously **sleep deprived** at six or fewer hours a night, says a 2011 study by the Centers for Disease Control and Prevention (CDC).

> **"You are more irrational when you're sleep deprived. Your emotions are much harder to control."**

It's a biological 1-2-3 punch. First, the onset of **puberty** brings a median 1.5-hour delay in the body's release of the sleep-inducing **hormone** melatonin, says Dr. Mary Carskadon, a professor of psychiatry and human behavior at the Brown University medical school and a leading sleep researcher.

Second, "sleep pressure," or the buildup of the need to sleep as the day wears on, slows during **adolescence**. That is, kids don't become sleepy as early. This sleep delay isn't just a passing impulse: it continues to increase through **adolescence**, peaking at age 19.5 in girls and age 20.9 in boys, Dr. Carskadon's research shows.

Finally, teens lose some of their sensitivity to morning light, the kind

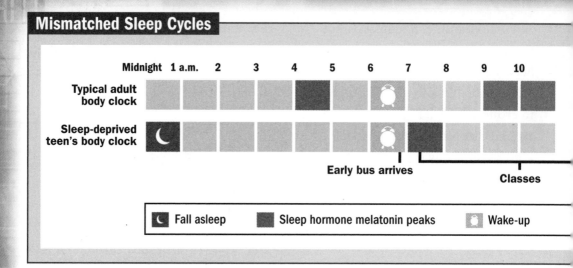

Mismatched Sleep Cycles

	Midnight	1 a.m.	2	3	4	5	6	7	8	9	10
Typical adult body clock											
Sleep-deprived teen's body clock											

Early bus arrives

Classes

🌙 Fall asleep   ■ Sleep hormone melatonin peaks   🕐 Wake-up

that spurs awakening and alertness. And they become more reactive to nighttime light, sparking activity later into the evening.

Dr. Carskadon says letting teens set their own schedules can lead to a downward spiral. Teens left to their own devices **tend to** cycle later, soaking up stimulating light from their computers. This can further delay sleep by 2½ to 3 hours.

Many parents feel defeated by schools' early start times. More than half of public high schools start before 8 a.m., according to a 2011 Brookings Institution study.

Maya Zimmerman's first class is at 7:20 a.m., and "when I wake up in the morning, I literally want to die," says the 16-year-old Falls Church, VA, high school junior. "I feel like it's the middle of the night and I don't feel like eating cereal." Ms. Zimmerman says she battles fatigue in class and often nods off while doing homework after school.

More than 35 schools or school districts in at least 21 states have delayed start times in recent years to allow teens to sleep longer, according to reports gathered by advocates. In Wake County, NC, where school start times were changed several times over a seven-year period, a one-hour delay was linked to an increase of three percentile points in middle school students' math and reading scores, according to a study published earlier this year in the *Economics of Education Review*.

Many schools, however, have rejected parental pressure to delay school starts, citing bus-cost savings, or the need to keep afternoons open for teens' sports or other activities.

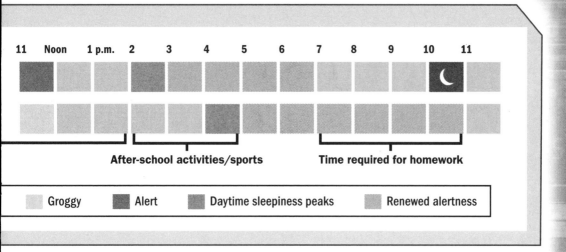

11	Noon	1 p.m.	2	3	4	5	6	7	8	9	10	11

After-school activities/sports   Time required for homework

Groggy   Alert   Daytime sleepiness peaks   Renewed alertness

Sleep loss is linked in research to decreases in memory, attention, and academic performance. Impaired functioning of the prefrontal cortex, which helps **regulate** sleep, has been detected in youngsters with attention **deficit** hyperactivity disorder.

Sleep-deprived teens are more likely to feel sad or hopeless, or to seriously consider suicide, according to a 2011 study by the CDC. A study published earlier this year by Dr. Carskadon and others links **sleep deprivation** in college freshmen to the expression of genetic **factors** linked to depression.

Still, most teens resist parents' setting bedtimes. Peer pressure plays a role. Teens with a friend who sleeps less than seven hours a night are 11 percent more likely to sleep less than seven

hours themselves, says a 2010 study in the science journal *PLoS ONE*.

Claude Albertario of Oceanside, New York, says his 15-year-old daughter, Rianna, stays up much too late, leaving her TV on through the night, "no matter my yelling." Rianna says she isn't sleepy until after midnight and usually falls asleep at 1 a.m. or 1:30 a.m., just five hours before she has to get up for school. She claims her TV helps her sleep by masking nighttime noises around the house.

An argument that does work with Rianna: citing research linking sleep loss in teens to obesity and other health problems. Knowing that more sleep will help her keep her skin clear and avoid gaining weight "motivates me more," says Rianna, who is trying gradually to move her bedtime up to midnight.

SHOULD NOT KNOWING ANOTHER LANGUAGE KEEP A DIPLOMA OUT OF REACH?

Data File

People who speak a second language can describe many benefits—for relationships, brain function, and college and job opportunities.

Learning Languages

- 25% of elementary schools, 58% of middle schools, and 91% of high schools offer foreign language instruction for students.
- Spanish is the most popular foreign language offered. The number of schools teaching French, German, Japanese, and Russian is decreasing. However, more schools are offering Arabic and Chinese.
- 8% of middle and high schools with language programs offer Spanish for Spanish speakers.

(Source: Center for Applied Linguistics, 2009)

Opening Doors to College

- 25% of four-year universities **require** students to have studied a language other than English in high school.
- 51% of four-year universities **require** students to study a foreign language to earn a degree.
- Native language speakers and other students can pass exams to meet either **requirement**.

(Source: Modern Language Association, 2012)

Talking Your Way to the CIA

- The Central Intelligence Agency offers an extra $35,000 to people who speak Arabic, Farsi, or Pashtu.
- Foreign Media Analysts earn $50,000–$97,000. Foreign Language Instructors earn even more.
- Employees receive additional pay rewards later in their careers if they keep up the language.

(Source: American Public Media, 2010)

MANY BENEFITS COME WITH LEARNING A FOREIGN LANGUAGE

by Kalli Damschen

Español. Français. Deutsch.

There are more than 6,000 languages in the world, and while many of these are not commonly taught and aren't spoken in most countries, students can reap a variety of **benefits**, both academic and personal, from studying any foreign language.

High school can be one of the very best times to learn a language. There are few other periods in life when you'll have as many opportunities to freely attend a class under the instruction of an experienced teacher.

Alyssa Gilbert, a sophomore at Bonneville High, hits on the most basic reason that studying a foreign language in high school is **beneficial**. She's taking Spanish "to get into college and (because) it helps to get a job."

More schools are offering Arabic, but the number is still small.

Most colleges now **require** that students have taken at least two years of the same foreign language in order to be **admitted**. Prestigious schools often have more stringent **requirements**. Stanford, for example, **requires** three or more years of a foreign language. Princeton expects four, while only **requiring** two years of both history and science. To many colleges, knowledge of a foreign language is at the very least attractive, and at the very most essential.

Many employers have a similar outlook. The ability to speak a foreign language can be very helpful in any job that deals with people, particularly in careers that have an international focus.

According to the *CIA World Factbook*, only 5.6 percent of the world's population speaks English as a **primary language**. There are hundreds of thousands of people who don't know English, making the ability to speak and write a different language a **valuable** commodity in many careers.

BENEFITS OVERFLOW

Alan Baggaley, a Spanish teacher at NUAMES, agrees.

"Learning Spanish, specifically, can open up many economic doors in our country such as in supervisory or managerial **capacities** and even international business," he says.

Most Widely Spoken Languages

LANGUAGE	NUMBER OF SPEAKERS	PERCENTAGE OF WORLD POPULATION
English	1,000,000,000	16%
Mandarin	1,000,000,000	16%
Hindi/Urdu	900,000,000	15%
Spanish	450,000,000	7%
Russian/Belarusian	320,000,000	5%
Arabic	250,000,000	4%
Bengali/Sylhetti	250,000,000	4%
Malay/Indonesian	200,000,000	3%
Portuguese	200,000,000	3%
Japanese	130,000,000	2%
French	125,000,000	2%
German	125,000,000	2%

Source: Encyclopædia Britannica, 2013

While Spanish is often useful with local and international jobs due to the large number of US residents who speak it, there are a variety of careers that **require** other foreign languages as well. Even if the job you're interested in doesn't **require bilingual** employees, the ability to speak a second language can make you a more **competitive** candidate for any job.

> THE ABILITY TO SPEAK A FOREIGN LANGUAGE CAN BE VERY HELPFUL IN ANY JOB THAT DEALS WITH PEOPLE.

The **benefits** of learning a foreign language can overflow into other academic areas as well. Studying a new language **requires** the development of a variety of skills that can be useful in and out of the classroom.

Bryan Andrews, a senior studying French at Northridge, says, "It's really hard because there are so many different verbs you have to learn. You have to have a lot of memorization skills and learn a lot of new concepts."

Foreign language classes foster abilities such as memorization and critical thinking that can improve academic performance in other subjects. Many studies suggest that students who learn a second language score significantly higher in areas such as math, reading comprehension, and language mechanics.

For instance, an analysis of more than 17,000 test scores by researchers Olsen and Brown revealed that high school students who studied a foreign language scored consistently higher on the English and mathematics portions of the ACT. Other studies have suggested similar results on the SAT as well.

"PARLEZ-VOUS FRANÇAIS?"

Apart from academic and employment **benefits**, taking a foreign language can open up a whole new array of opportunities in traveling. Language is an essential part of a country's **culture**, and you can experience another **culture** much better when you can converse with the people and understand where they come from.

"I like Mandarin Chinese because each word carries such a great amount of history behind it. They evolved and changed," says Christal Hazelton, a junior at Clearfield High.

A language often tells a lot about a country's **culture** and heritage, enabling a better understanding of the people who speak it. Aside from that, foreign language classes often teach more than just the language, touching on things such as geography, food, and traditions.

Andrews says his favorite part of French class is the different **cultures** that he gets to experience, such as Mardi Gras.

Mikayla Coy, a sophomore at Bonneville, agrees, saying that she loves that she gets to "learn about how other people live and speak."

"A NEW LENS"

Bilingualism can also lead to better relationships with people from foreign countries.

"I want to be able to **communicate** with people who don't speak English," Coy, who's studying Spanish and American Sign Language, says.

Zach Griffin, a sophomore at Syracuse, says that this is his favorite part of studying Chinese—being able to speak with people in the different language.

Language is the key component of **communication**; being unable to speak another's language can build barriers between relationships and prevent you from fully understanding someone's meaning. While translators can bridge the language barrier, being able to speak with someone personally is important for building a relationship.

All in all, learning a foreign language can be a great opportunity. Not only can it broaden your horizons and help you to look beyond the familiar, at the same time it can teach you to take a step back and examine your own **culture** and ways of **communication**.

"Learning another language enables students to see the world through a new lens," says Baggaley. "The human race no longer lives in secluded homogeneous groups, but as a world community. Developing skills in understanding, appreciating, and even participating in some aspects of another **culture** is paramount to success in our day."

Foreign languages can open thousands of doors when it comes to college, careers, and travel, and can lead to new friendships—or, as they would say in Spanish class—nuevos amigos!

Kalli Damschen is a junior at Clearfield High School, TX.

THE EFFECTS OF A SECOND LANGUAGE ON THE BRAIN

by Andrianes Pinantoan

1 In this day and age of increasing **global** interconnectivity, having the ability to speak more than one language is a highly **valued** skill. Studying a foreign language is a **requirement** in some schools in the United States, but in some countries, it's the law that all students pass two languages before they are allowed to graduate.

Meanwhile, those who grew up learning only English are taking language classes in droves.

There is a reason, of course. **Bilingualism** can very well translate to better job opportunities and better pay. In some career paths, fluency in more than one language is an absolute **requirement**. And who can resist the temptation to brag about being able to speak French?

So imagine my surprise when I read that the scientific community used to believe **bilingualism** was bad for your brain. In his 1993 book, *Foundations of Bilingual Education and Bilingualism*, Dr. Colin Baker, professor of Education at Bangor University, wrote that around a century ago, it was believed that **bilingualism** could cause language confusion ("cerebral confusion"), "split personality," and even spiritual decline.

Several states require students to take a foreign language to graduate from high school.

He then followed up with his 1995 book, *A Parents' and Teachers' Guide to Bilingualism*, and noted that just half a century ago, educators across North America used to discourage immigrant parents from using their native language at home. Practicing a second language, it was believed, could hamper children's ability to absorb formal education.

The underlying argument for this belief was that the brain was limited in its **capacity**. So in learning a new language, the brain had to sacrifice some of its working **capacity**. Using the metaphor of a weighing scale, it was argued that the study of a second language would reduce the brain's **capacity** to **retain** knowledge of the other language.

That era is long gone.

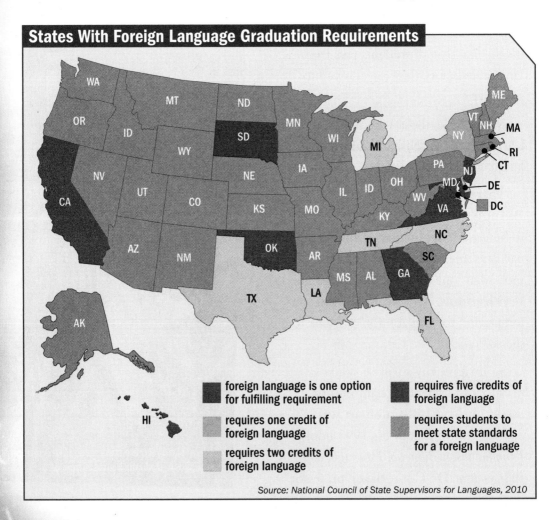

States With Foreign Language Graduation Requirements

- foreign language is one option for fulfilling requirement
- requires one credit of foreign language
- requires two credits of foreign language
- requires five credits of foreign language
- requires students to meet state standards for a foreign language

Source: National Council of State Supervisors for Languages, 2010

❷ Many researchers have since dispelled the misconceptions surrounding the disadvantages of learning a second language. Janet Werker from the University of British Columbia, for example, compared babies who grew up in **bilingual** homes and those in monolingual homes.

> EACH YEAR OF FOREIGN LANGUAGE STUDY CORRELATED WITH HIGHER VERBAL AND MATH SCORES ON THE SAT.

She found that babies from **bilingual** homes were able to distinguish between different languages, while those from monolingual homes could not—showing that language confusion doesn't occur when children learn more than one language early in their lives.

In fact, various experiments since then have shown that the study of foreign languages is linked to various **cognitive** advantages. Dumas, for example, reported in the journal *Child* that the study of foreign language did not induce language confusion, and it even improved students' English language skills.

In the study that involved 13,200 students in third and fourth grades of Louisiana public schools, students who studied a foreign language **invariably** did better on the English portion of the Louisiana Basic Skill tests than those who did not—regardless of their race, gender, or academic level.

And if you think only young children **benefit** from learning a second language, consider the study conducted by T. C. Cooper and published in *The Modern Language Journal* (1987). Cooper analyzed the data collected from the Admission Testing Program of the College Board and found that students who studied a foreign language in high school had better SAT scores, and that each year of foreign language study correlated with higher verbal and math scores on the SAT.

While those who did not study a foreign language had a mean of 366 on the verbal SAT and 409 on the math SAT, those with one year of foreign language scored slightly higher (378 and 416) and those with five years of foreign language scored dramatically higher (504 and 535).

ENRICHING THE BRAIN

Dr. Colin Baker challenged the earlier hypothesis that suggested our brain has a limited **capacity** for the **acquisition** of a new language. He also challenged the idea that different languages are **retained** in different parts of the brain. (The belief was that the brain was sectioned into exclusive parts containing the knowledge of one language and with no **communication** or overlapping among the exclusive sections.) He argued that the knowledge of different languages is not kept apart. Instead, they are meshed together in our **cognitive** systems, and readily transferred and generalized into one another to enrich and add to the collective knowledge.

Therefore, Baker reasoned, **bilingualism** could boost your **cognitive** skills.

He further suggested that by knowing different words in different languages to describe one particular object or idea, the brain of a **bilingual** person possesses an increased flexibility in **cognitive** thinking.

Baker also found that **bilingual** children showed higher creativity in storytelling, which was supported by Ianco-Worrall's research that revealed that **bilingual** children were ahead of their monolingual peers in terms of semantic language development by two to three years!

> THE BRAIN OF A BILINGUAL PERSON POSSESSES AN INCREASED FLEXIBILITY IN COGNITIVE THINKING.

Could it be that smarter students simply preferred to take up another language? Diaz studied this issue in depth, and using statistical analysis he was able to determine that the causal link runs from **bilingualism** to increased **cognitive** ability—lending support to Baker's theory.

❸ BETTER BRAIN STRUCTURES

If statistical analysis and theories aren't enough, consider this experiment.

In an attempt to learn more about the correlation of learning a second language and its effect on the brain, Andrea Mechelli and colleagues of London's Wellcome Department of Imaging Neuroscience, along with experts from Fondazione Santa Lucia in Rome, administered a brain imaging experiment on three groups of people. The first group was monolingual, the second group learned a second language before the age of five, and the third group learned a second language by the ages of 10 to 15.

The experiment showed that **bilingual** participants had denser brain tissues compared to monolingual ones. Brain tissues that showed as being denser were specifically gray matter, the tissue that makes up most of the brain's nervous cells.

This increased density was more apparent in the left hemisphere of the brain—the area responsible for language and **communication** skills—but was still observable in the **bilingual** participants' right hemispheres. (This supported the notion that learning a second language is not merely a **linguistic** activity, but also a **cognitive** activity of the brain.)

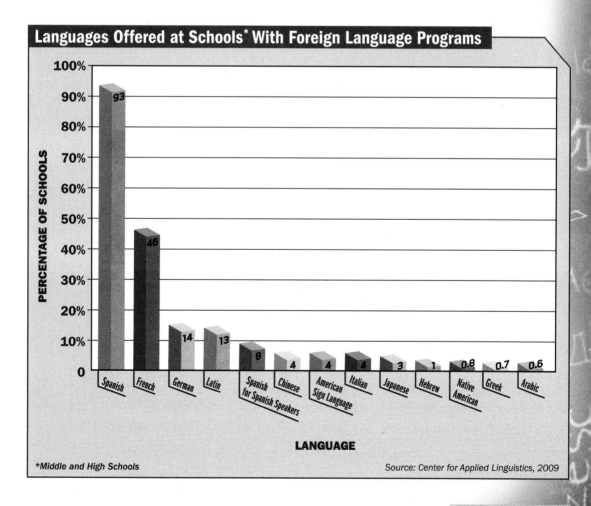

Languages Offered at Schools* With Foreign Language Programs

PERCENTAGE OF SCHOOLS

Spanish 93, French 46, German 14, Latin 13, Spanish for Spanish Speakers 8, Chinese 4, American Sign Language 4, Italian 4, Japanese 3, Hebrew 1, Native American 0.8, Greek 0.7, Arabic 0.6

LANGUAGE

*Middle and High Schools

Source: Center for Applied Linguistics, 2009

Children who learn more than one language before age five have denser gray matter than those who learn a second language later in life.

The study also found that the group who **acquired** a second language early in life (before age five) had denser gray matter in the brain imaging experiment compared to the group who **acquired** a second language later in life.

The researchers who published this study in the journal *Nature* concluded that studying a second language may possibly alter the structure of the human brain, and that the earlier the learning **acquisition** process began, the greater the **impact** in the brain's gray matter density.

What the experiment above suggests is that **bilinguals** may have a **cognitive** advantage over their monolingual peers due to better brain structures, namely the gray matter, that are more actively developed as they learn a second language, especially when they start early in childhood.

> BILINGUALS MAY HAVE A COGNITIVE ADVANTAGE OVER THEIR MONOLINGUAL PEERS DUE TO BETTER BRAIN STRUCTURES.

BUILDING A COGNITIVE RESERVE IN THE BRAIN

So far we've covered how **bilingualism benefits** children and teenagers. What about the elders? Well, experts now believe that learning a second language can help slow the onset of Alzheimer's and dementia by increasing the brain's **cognitive** reserve.

Kovelman, together with other researchers, conducted an experiment that suggests **bilingualism** encourages the brain to build a **cognitive** reserve. He found that, while different languages were processed in much of the same area of the brain (in the left hemisphere), there's nonetheless increased activity in the right hemisphere when participants switch back and forth between two languages.

These increased activities particularly took place in part of the brain called the "dorsolateral prefrontal cortex," an area responsible for working memory, organization, regulation, and intellectual function, among others. (Mechelli, whose findings are discussed previously, came to the same conclusion.)

This expansion of neural activity outside of its common area when the speaker is in **bilingual** mode is as predictable as it is prominent on **bilingual** people's brain scans, such that this phenomenon is often dubbed as **bilingualism's** "neurological signature." The purpose of the neurological signature, experts argue, is to maximize the **communication** effectiveness of both languages.

Learning a second language, in other words, is to the brain like what exercise is to the body. It keeps the brain healthy and strong because it's a **cognitively** challenging task.

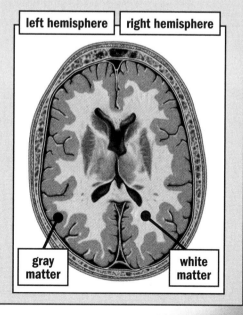

The Bilingual Brain

- Bilinguals have denser gray matter, especially in the left hemisphere.
- People who speak two languages have more activity in the right hemisphere when they switch between languages.
- Learning a second language can slow the onset of Alzheimer's disease and dementia.

left hemisphere | right hemisphere

gray matter

white matter

BILINGUAL/BILINGÜE

by Rhina P. Espaillat

My father liked them separate, one there
one here (allá y aquí), as if aware

that words might cut in two his daughter's heart
(el corazón) and lock the alien part

to what he was—his memory, his name
(su nombre)—with a key he could not claim.

"English outside this door, Spanish inside,"
he said, "y basta." But who can divide

the world, the word (mundo y palabra) from
any child? I knew how to be dumb

and stubborn (testaruda); late, in bed,
I hoarded secret syllables I read

until my tongue (mi lengua) learned to run
where his stumbled. And still the heart was one.

I like to think he knew that, even when,
proud (orgulloso) of his daughter's pen,

he stood outside mis versos, half in fear
of words he loved but wanted not to hear.

Glosario español/Spanish Glossary

allá: there

aquí: here

bilingüe: bilingual

el corazón: the heart

mi lengua: my tongue

mis versos: my verses

mundo y palabra: world and word

orgulloso: proud

su nombre: his name

testaruda: stubborn

y basta: and enough

Meet the Author

RHINA P. ESPAILLAT

Born: January 20, 1932, in the Dominican Republic. Immigrated to the United States in 1939 because her father opposed the dictator, Rafael Trujillo

College: Hunter College and Queens College, both in New York City

Books: "Bilingual/Bilingüe" is from *Where Horizons Go*, which won the T. S. Eliot Prize in 1998. Her 10 other collections include *Rehearsing Absence*, *The Shadow I Dress In*, and *El olor de la memoria/The Scent of Memory*.

In Her Own Words: "Poems occur to me in one language or the other for no reason I can fathom. But they do arrive most often in English, which is, after all, the language in which most of my life has been lived. I began translating them back and forth some years ago, in order to share them with friends and family on both sides of the language divide."

Are teens old enough to get behind the wheel?

Data File

Car crashes are the leading cause of death for teens in the United States, so it's no wonder many states are buckling down on teen driving restrictions.

Driving While Distracted

- In 2011, 3,331 people were killed in crashes **involving** a **distracted** driver.
- 40% of American teenagers say they have been in a car when the driver used a cell phone in a way that put people in danger.
- 11% of drivers under the age of 20 **involved** in fatal crashes were reported as **distracted** at the time.

(Source: Distraction.gov, 2013)

Risky Business

Among teen drivers, those at especially high **risk** for motor vehicle crashes are:

- Males—In 2010, the motor vehicle death rate for 16- to 19-year-old males was almost twice as high as the motor vehicle death rate for females the same age.
- Teens driving with teen passengers—Having teen passengers in the car increases the crash **risk** of **unsupervised** teen drivers. The more passengers, the higher the **risk**.
- Newly licensed teens—The **risk** of crashing is highest during the first few months of having a license.

(Source: Centers for Disease Control and Prevention, 2012)

Graduated Driving Laws

Most states enacted Graduated Driver Licensing (GDL) programs during the 1990s with three stages:

- Learner Stage—**supervised** driving, cumulating with a driver's test
- Intermediate Stage—limiting **unsupervised** driving in **high-risk** situations
- Full Privilege Stage—a standard driver's license

(Source: Governors Highway Safety Association, 2013)

DN'T TXT N DRV

Why you should disconnect while driving

by Nancy Mann Jackson

When Wil Craig tells his story, teens listen. In 2008, when he was an Indiana high school senior, Craig was riding in his girlfriend's car as she drove and texted at the same time. **Distracted**, she wrecked the car.

The driver had no serious injuries. But Craig suffered a collapsed lung, four broken ribs, and a traumatic brain injury. He spent eight weeks in a coma. After he learned to walk and talk again and eventually returned to school, Craig began sharing his story with other teenagers—so far more than 10,000—to help stop teen texting and driving.

Widespread Damage

There are many more people who need to hear Craig's message. Driver **distraction** has become a national problem, especially because cell phone use has increased. Look around the next time you're on the road (as a passenger, of course), and see how many drivers are talking or texting on their cell phones. That can lead them to take their focus off the road and cause serious, even fatal, accidents.

Nearly 28 percent of all vehicle crashes, or about 1.6 million each year, can be linked to talking on a cell phone or texting while driving, the National Safety Council estimates. The problem is especially dire for US teens: Among those ages 16 and 17, some 26 percent have texted from behind the wheel. (And 43 percent of those in that age group admitted talking on a cell phone while driving, according to a Pew Internet & American Life Project study.)

Nearly 26 percent of 16- and 17-year-olds admit to texting while driving.

Thirty-one states have restrictions for teen drivers, including bans on using phones while driving.

Why Cells and Driving Don't Mix

While there are many activities that can **distract** a driver, such as eating or adjusting the radio while driving (see "Driven to Distraction"), sending text messages may be the worst. "Texting is among the most dangerous activities for drivers because it **involves** taking your eyes and attention off the roadway," says Justin McNaull, director of state relations for AAA, formerly known as the American Automobile Association. "Even taking your eyes off the road for two seconds doubles your chances of being in a crash."

Not convinced? Stats from a Federal Motor Carrier Safety Administration study tell the story:

- Compared with 16 other **distracting** activities, texting had the highest odds of causing a serious crash.

- Drivers who were texting were 23.2 times more likely to crash than those drivers who weren't texting.

- When texting, drivers took their eyes off the road for an average of 4.6 seconds.

Likewise, making phone calls, even with a hands-free headset, while driving is more dangerous than speaking to a passenger. That's because a passenger will pause in conversation when the driver needs to concentrate on the road. "Even in conversation, an adult passenger can appreciate when the driver is doing something more demanding, like merging onto the highway," McNaull says. "Someone on a cell phone doesn't know or appreciate what the driver's doing."

Only 2 percent of people are able to safely multitask while driving, estimates David Strayer, a psychology professor at the University of Utah. He has studied the effects that cell phone use while driving has on the brain. Even though teens are more likely to try multitasking, they're part of that 98 percent who can't do it safely, Strayer says. Driving is a new skill for teens, so doing multiple things simultaneously takes more effort for them than for more **experienced** drivers.

What the Law Says

As the **risks** of texting while driving have become more obvious, lawmakers across the country have begun to take notice—and to take action.

- Currently, laws in 30 states and the District of Columbia make it illegal to text or send email while driving.

- Eight states plus the District of Columbia completely **ban** the use of a handheld phone while driving.

- Thirty-one states have separate **restrictions** for teens, including **bans** on using phones while driving or texting while driving.

The penalties for breaking those laws range from fines to jail time. On the federal level, texting while driving has been **banned** for interstate truck drivers, and Congress is considering several bills that would encourage all states to pass laws **banning** texting while driving.

An Ounce of Prevention

Whether calling or texting while driving is **restricted** by law, smart drivers are rethinking the use of phones behind the wheel. However, it can be tough to ditch the phone. "People have a real desire to be connected and have the immediate ability to keep in touch with friends and family," McNaull says. "Giving up texting and talking on the phone while driving is hard."

> **"EVEN TAKING YOUR EYES OFF THE ROAD FOR TWO SECONDS DOUBLES YOUR CHANCES OF BEING IN A CRASH."**

To avoid the temptation, McNaull recommends simply turning off your phone and putting it away before getting behind the wheel. Talk to your parents, and let them know that if you don't respond to their phone calls or texts right away, it's because you're driving. Avoid calling or texting your friends if you know they're driving at the time.

Some teens even use technology to help them avoid texting while driving. Zach Veach is a 15-year-old who races cars for Andretti Autosport. He began speaking out after a teen who had been driving for only two months was killed while texting in an accident near his home in Ohio. To help other teens,

Zach developed urTXT, an application for smart phones that sends an auto response to the sender of a text, letting the sender know that the recipient is driving and will respond later.

Safe Alternatives

Like Zach, many teens are finding ways they can make a difference. Nebraska teen Emily Reynolds says texting and driving was once a big problem among her friends. After her older sister, Cady, was killed in a crash at age 16, Emily's family started the C. A. R. Alliance for Safer Teen Driving (named for the initials of Cady Anne Reynolds). The group visits schools to share the dangers of **distracted** driving with those who are just beginning to drive.

Since the C. A. R. presentation at her school, Emily says, she's seen fewer and fewer classmates texting while driving. When she finds herself in a car with another teen who is texting, Emily, who's now 17, doesn't hesitate to speak up. "I will absolutely say something, and it is usually along the lines of, 'You really shouldn't do that while you drive. Would you like me to text someone for you?'" she says. "Offering to do it for them gives a good **alternative**, and it gets the point across."

Zach goes even further. "The first time I see [other people] do it, I tell them that I don't want to lose my life and they don't know how dangerous texting and driving is," he says. "Most people tell me they do it all the time and nothing has happened. [If] they refuse [to stop], I turn their car off and take the keys until they agree to put the phone down."

Extreme? Maybe. But separating driving from cell phone use is a way to make sure crashes such as the one that forever changed Wil Craig's life never happen again.

Driven to Distraction

Using a cell phone to talk or text isn't the only safety risk behind the wheel, says Emily Reynolds, a 17-year-old whose sister died in an accident that Emily believes was caused by a distracted driver.

"Anything from putting on makeup to one other person being in your car and everything in between is a huge distraction that people do not realize."

Behaviors to avoid while driving include:

- **Eating**
- **Arguing with a passenger**
- **Putting on makeup**
- **Reading or writing**
- **Searching for an item in the vehicle**

Is 16 Too Young to Drive a Car?

by Robert Davis

Raise the driving age. That radical idea is gaining momentum in the fight to save the lives of teenage drivers, the most dangerous on the USA's roads, and their passengers.

Brain and auto safety experts fear that 16-year-olds, the youngest drivers licensed in most states, are too **immature** to handle today's cars and roadway **risks**.

New findings from brain researchers at the National Institutes of Health explain for the first time why efforts to protect the youngest drivers usually fail. The weak link: what's called "the executive branch" of the teen brain, the part that weighs **risks**, makes judgments, and controls **impulsive** behavior.

❶ Scientists at the NIH campus in Bethesda, Maryland, have found that this vital area develops through the teenage years and isn't fully **mature** until age 25. One 16-year-old's

Safety researchers believe that it's immaturity, and not inexperience, that causes many teen drivers to crash.

brain might be more developed than another 18-year-old's, just as a younger teen might be taller than an older one. But evidence is mounting that a 16-year-old's brain is generally far less developed than those of teens just a little older.

The research seems to help explain why 16-year-old drivers crash at far higher rates than older teens. The studies have convinced a growing number of safety experts that 16-year-olds are too young to drive safely without **supervision**.

"Privately, a lot of people in safety think it's a good idea to raise the driving age," says Barbara Harsha, executive director of the Governors Highway Safety Association. "It's a topic that is emerging."

Americans increasingly favor raising the driving age, a USA TODAY/CNN/Gallup Poll has found. Nearly two-thirds—61 percent—say they think a 16-year-old is too young to have a driver's license. Only 37 percent of those polled thought it was okay to license 16-year-olds, compared with 50 percent who thought so in 1995.

A slight majority, 53 percent, think teens should be at least 18 to get a license.

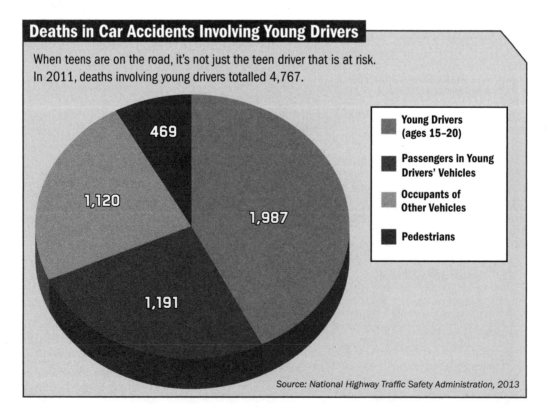

Deaths in Car Accidents Involving Young Drivers

When teens are on the road, it's not just the teen driver that is at risk. In 2011, deaths involving young drivers totalled 4,767.

- Young Drivers (ages 15–20)
- Passengers in Young Drivers' Vehicles
- Occupants of Other Vehicles
- Pedestrians

469
1,120
1,987
1,191

Source: National Highway Traffic Safety Administration, 2013

The poll of 1,002 adults, **conducted** Dec. 17–19, 2004, has an error margin of +/-3 percentage points.

Many states have begun to raise the age by **imposing restrictions** on 16-year-old drivers. Examples: limiting the number of passengers they can carry or barring late-night driving. But the idea of flatly forbidding 16-year-olds to drive without parental **supervision**—as New Jersey does—has run into resistance from many lawmakers and parents around the country.

Irving Slosberg, a Florida state representative who lost his 14-year-old daughter in a 1995 crash, says that when he proposed a law to raise the driving age, other lawmakers "laughed at me."

Bill Van Tassel, AAA's national manager of driving training programs, hears both sides of the argument. "We have parents who are pretty much tired of chauffeuring their kids around, and they want their children to be able to drive," he says. "Driving is a very emotional issue."

But safety experts fear inaction could lead to more young lives lost. Some sound a note of urgency about changing course. The reason: A record number of American teenagers will soon be behind the wheel as the peak of the "baby boomlet" hits driving age.

Already, on average, two people die every day across the USA in vehicles driven by 16-year-old drivers. One in five 16-year-olds will have a reportable car crash within the first year.

> ## ONE IN FIVE 16-YEAR-OLDS WILL HAVE A REPORTABLE CAR CRASH WITHIN THE FIRST YEAR.

In 2003, there were 937 drivers age 16 who were **involved** in fatal crashes. In those wrecks, 411 of the 16-year-old drivers died and 352 of their passengers were killed. Sixteen-year-old drivers are **involved** in fatal crashes at a rate nearly five times the rate of drivers 20 or older.

Gayle Bell, whose 16-year-old daughter, Jessie, rolled her small car into a Missouri ditch and died in July 2003, says she used to happily be Jessie's "ride." She would give anything for the chance to drive Jessie again.

"We were always together, but not as much after she got her license," Bell says. "If I could bring her back, I'd lasso the moon."

❷ Most states have focused their fixes on giving teens more driving **experience** before granting them **unrestricted** licenses. But the new brain research suggests that a separate factor is just as crucial: **maturity**. A new 17- or 18-year-old driver is considered safer than a new 16-year-old driver.

Even some teens are **acknowledging** that 16-year-olds are generally not ready to face the life-threatening **risks** that drivers can encounter behind the wheel.

"Raising the driving age from 16 to 17 would benefit society as a whole," says Liza Darwin, 17, of Nashville. Though many parents would be **inconvenienced** and teens would be frustrated, she says, "It makes sense to raise the driving age to save more lives."

States With Driving Restrictions

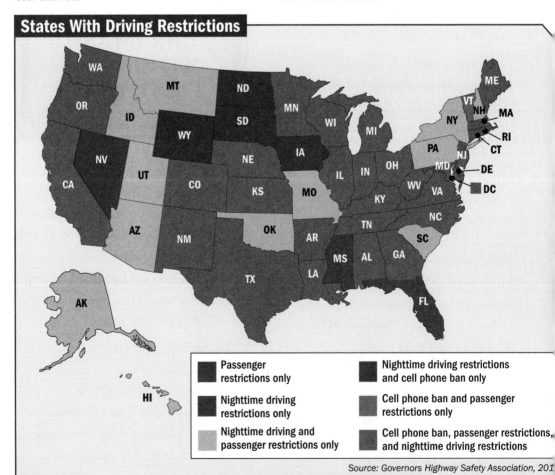

Legend:
- Passenger restrictions only
- Nighttime driving restrictions only
- Nighttime driving and passenger restrictions only
- Nighttime driving restrictions and cell phone ban only
- Cell phone ban and passenger restrictions only
- Cell phone ban, passenger restrictions, and nighttime driving restrictions

Source: Governors Highway Safety Association, 201

Focus on Lawmakers

But those in a position to raise the driving age—legislators in states throughout the USA— have mostly refused to do so.

Adrienne Mandel, a Maryland state legislator, has tried since 1997 to pass tougher teen driving laws. Even lawmakers who recognize that a higher driving age could save lives, Mandel notes, resist the notion of having to drive their 16-year-olds to after-school activities that the teens could drive to themselves.

"Other delegates said, 'What are you doing? You're going to make me drive my kid to the movies on Friday night for another six months?'" Mandel says. "Parents are talking about **inconvenience**, and I'm talking about saving lives."

Yet the USA TODAY poll found that among the general public, majorities in both suburbs (65 percent) and urban areas (60 percent) favor licensing ages above 16.

While a smaller percentage in rural areas (54 percent) favor raising the driving age, experts say it's striking that majority support exists even there, considering that teens on farms often start driving very young to help with workloads.

For those who oppose raising the minimum age, their argument is often this: Responsible teen drivers shouldn't be punished for the mistakes of the small fraction who cause deadly crashes.

The debate stirs images of reckless teens drag racing or driving drunk. But such flagrant misdeeds account for only a small portion of the fatal actions of 16-year-old drivers. Only about 10 percent of the 16-year-old drivers killed in 2003 had blood-alcohol concentrations of 0.10 or higher, compared with 43 percent of 20- to 49-year-old drivers killed, according to the Insurance Institute for Highway Safety.

Instead, most fatal crashes with 16-year-old drivers (77 percent) **involved** driver errors, especially the kind most common among novices. Examples: speeding, overcorrecting after veering off the road, and losing control when facing a roadway obstacle that a more **mature** driver would be more likely to handle safely. That's the highest percentage of error for any age group.

For years, researchers suspected that **inexperience**—the bane of any new driver—was mostly to blame for deadly crashes **involving** teens. When trouble arose, the theory went, the young driver simply made the wrong move. But in recent years, safety researchers have noticed a pattern emerge—one that seems to stem more from **immaturity** than from **inexperience**.

> **"WE HAVE PARENTS WHO ARE PRETTY MUCH TIRED OF CHAUFFEURING THEIR KIDS AROUND."**

"Skills are a minor factor in most cases," says Allan Williams, former chief scientist at the insurance institute. "It's really attitudes and emotions."

A peek inside the brain

The NIH brain research suggests that the problem is human biology. A crucial part of the teen's brain—the area that peers ahead and considers consequences—remains undeveloped. That means careless attitudes and rash emotions often drive teen decisions, says Jay Giedd, chief of brain imaging in the child psychiatric unit at the National Institute of Mental Health, who's leading the study.

"It all comes down to **impulse** control," Giedd says. "The brain is changing a lot longer than we used to think. And that part of the brain **involved** in decision-making and controlling **impulses** is among the latest to come on board."

The teen brain is a paradox. Some areas—those that control senses, reactions and physical abilities—are fully developed in teenagers. "Physically, they should be ruling the world," Giedd says. "But (adolescence) is not that great of a time emotionally."

Giedd and an international research team have analyzed 4,000 brain scans from 2,000 volunteers to document how brains evolve as children **mature**.

In his office at the NIH, Giedd points to an image of a brain on his computer screen that illustrates brain development from childhood to adulthood. As he sets the time lapse in motion, the brain turns blue rapidly in some areas and more slowly in others. One area that's slow to turn blue—which represents development over time—is the right side just over the temple. It's the spot on the head where a parent might tap a frustrated finger while asking his teen, "What were you thinking?"

This underdeveloped area is called the dorsal lateral prefrontal cortex. The underdeveloped blue on Giedd's screen is where thoughts of long-term consequences spring to consciousness. And in teen after teen, the research team found, it's not fully **mature**.

"This is the top rung," Giedd says. "This is the part of the brain that, in a sense, associates everything. All of our hopes and dreams for the future. All of our memories of the past. Our values. Everything going on in our environment. Everything to make a decision."

When a smart, talented and very **mature** teen does something a parent might call "stupid," Giedd says, it's this underdeveloped part of the brain that has most likely failed.

"That's the part of the brain that helps look farther ahead," he says. "In a sense, increasing the time between **impulse** and decisions. It seems not to get as good as it's going to get until age 25."

❸ This slow process plays a kind of dirty trick on teens, whose hormones are churning. As their bodies turn more adultlike, the hormones encourage more **risk-taking** and thrill-seeking. That might be nature's way of helping them leave the nest. But as the hormones fire up the part of the brain that responds to pleasure, known as the limbic system, emotions run high. Those emotions

make it hard to quickly form wise judgments—the kind drivers must make every day.

That's also why teens often seem more impetuous than adults. In making decisions, they rely more on the parts of their brain that control emotion. They're "hotter" when angry and "colder" when sad, Giedd says.

When a teen is traveling 15 to 20 miles per hour over the speed limit, the part of his or her brain that processes a thrill is working brilliantly. But the part that warns of negative consequences? It's all but useless.

"It may not seem that fast to them," Giedd says, because they're not weighing the same factors an adult might. They're not asking themselves,

Brain Development

frontal lobes

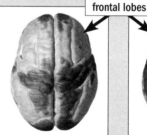 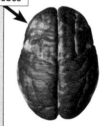

MRI of Teen Brain:
The yellow, red, and green areas show ongoing development.

MRI of Adult Brain:
The frontal lobes in the cerebral cortex are among the last areas to mature.

The undeveloped "executive branch" of the teen brain makes it difficult for teens to weigh risks, make judgments, and control impulsive behavior.

Source: *National Institute of Mental Health, 2004*

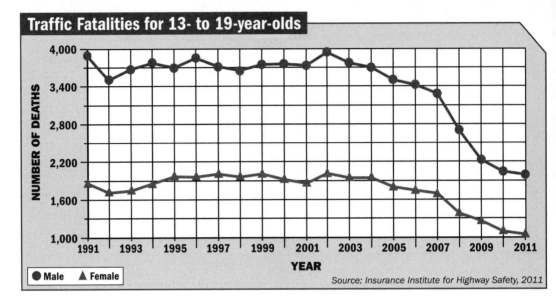

Traffic Fatalities for 13- to 19-year-olds

NUMBER OF DEATHS

YEAR

● Male ▲ Female

Source: Insurance Institute for Highway Safety, 2011

he says, "'Should I go fast or not?' And dying is not really part of the equation."

Precisely how brain development plays out on the roads has yet to be studied. Giedd says brain scans of teens in driving simulations might tell researchers exactly what's going on in their heads. That could lead to better training and a clearer understanding of which teens are ready to make critical driving decisions.

In theory, a teen's brain could eventually be scanned to determine whether he or she was neurologically fit to drive. But Giedd says that ethical crossroad is too radical to seriously consider today. "We are just at the threshold of this," he says.

Finding Explanations

The new insights into the teen brain might help explain why efforts

to protect young drivers, ranging from driver education to laws that **restrict** teen driving, have had only modest success. With the judgment center of the teen brain not fully developed, parents and states must struggle to instill decision-making skills in still-**immature** drivers.

In nearly every state, 16-year-old drivers face limits known as "graduated licensing" rules. These **restrictions** vary. But typically, they bar 16-year-olds from carrying other teen passengers, driving at night, or driving alone until they have driven a certain number of hours under parental **supervision**.

These states have, in effect, already raised their driving age. Safety experts say lives have been saved as a result. But it's mostly left to parents to **enforce** the **restrictions**, and the evidence suggests **enforcement** has been weak.

Teens probably appear to their parents at the dinner table to be more in control than they are behind the wheel. They might recite perfectly the **risks** of speeding, drinking and driving, or **distractions**, such as carrying passengers or talking on a cell phone, Giedd says. But their brains are built to learn more from example.

For teenagers, years of watching parents drive after downing a few glasses of wine or while chatting on a cell phone might make a deeper imprint than a lecture from a driver education teacher.

The brain research raises this question: How well can teen brains respond to the stresses of driving?

More research on teen driving decisions is needed, safety **advocates** say, before definitive conclusions can be drawn. And more public support is probably needed before politicians would seriously consider raising the driving age.

In the 1980s, Congress pressured states to raise their legal age to buy alcohol to 21. The goal was to stop teens from crossing borders to buy alcohol, after reports of drunken teens dying in auto crashes. Fueled by groups such as Mothers Against Drunk Driving, public support for stricter laws grew until Congress forced a rise in the drinking age.

> IT'S MOSTLY LEFT TO PARENTS TO ENFORCE THE RESTRICTIONS, AND THE EVIDENCE SUGGESTS ENFORCEMENT HAS BEEN WEAK.

Those laws have saved an estimated 20,000 lives in the past 20 years. Yet safety **advocates** say politicians remain generally unwilling to raise the driving age.

"If this were forced on the states, it would not be accepted very well," Harsha says. "What it usually takes for politicians to change their minds is a series of crashes involving young people. When enough of those kinds of things happen, then politicians are more likely to be open to other suggestions.

Unsafe Behind the Wheel?

With car crashes the leading cause of death for teenagers, states are placing greater restrictions on young drivers.

by Kate Zernike

It's long been a rite of passage for American teens: getting a driver's license and going for a spin with as many friends as can cram into the car.

But with mounting evidence that teenagers are at high **risk** for car accidents, more states are legislating away that carefree cruise, **imposing** tougher **restrictions** on how and when teens can drive—and who they can take along for the ride.

Fifteen states and Washington, DC, now prohibit **unsupervised** teenagers in their probationary period from driving with another teenager, and 44 states forbid them from driving with more than one teen. In South Carolina, teenagers can't drive after

Most drivers must pass a driving test before getting their full license.

6 p.m. in winter (8 p.m. in summer), and in Idaho, they're **banned** from driving from sundown to sunup.

In New Jersey—which has long had the nation's highest licensing age, 17—lawmakers have pushed further. New Jersey now requires first-year drivers under 21 to attach a red decal to their license plates to make it easier for the police to **enforce** an 11 p.m. curfew and passenger **restrictions**. And a bill now before the state legislature would require parents of teen drivers to complete a driver education course.

Safety campaigners point to studies showing that teen driving laws have significantly reduced traffic deaths.

But others, like Jeffrey Nadel, the 19-year-old president of the National Youth Rights Association, take issue with driving **restrictions**.

"These laws are blatantly discriminatory," says Nadel. He also argues they may have an unintended downside: A 2011 study in *The Journal of the American Medical Association* suggests that **restrictions** for young drivers may lead to a higher **incidence** of fatal accidents for 18-year-olds, possibly because they didn't get enough practical driving **experience** earlier.

Lawmakers around the nation, however, say the **restrictions** are necessary in light of some alarming statistics: Car crashes are the leading cause of death for teenagers, who have a crash rate four times higher than that of older drivers.

> **CAR CRASHES ARE THE LEADING CAUSE OF DEATH FOR TEENAGERS, WHO HAVE A CRASH RATE FOUR TIMES HIGHER THAN THAT OF OLDER DRIVERS.**

Texting Behind the Wheel

Studies have shown that teens tend to overrate their driving skills and underrate **risks** on the road. They also have more trouble multitasking—talking to friends, listening to the radio, and texting are particularly hazardous. Teenage drivers' **risk** of a crash increases 44 percent with one teenage passenger and quadruples with three or more. Two-thirds of teen passenger deaths happen in a car driven by another teen.

Efforts to address the dangers of teen driving date back to the mid-1990s. Starting with Florida, states began passing laws providing for "graduated driver's licenses" that require teenagers to undergo periods of **supervision** and probation before getting a full license.

Now, all states have graduated driver's licensing. And most are moving toward tougher **restrictions** on young drivers, including passenger limits, tighter curfews, and **bans** on cell phone use, even with headsets. Some states are also tying driving privileges to school attendance. These kinds of **restrictions** generally do not apply to new drivers over 21.

This summer, Congress got **involved**, offering highway safety grants to states that strengthen teen driving laws and crack down on texting-and-driving for all ages: **distracted** driving was a factor in at least 3,000 deaths in 2010.

Efforts have been particularly aggressive in the bumper-to-bumper Northeast. Bills requiring a decal for drivers under 21 are pending in the New York and Rhode Island legislatures. They come on the heels of New Jersey's "Kyleigh's Law," which took effect in 2010. The law is named for Kyleigh D'Alessio, a

16-year-old killed in a car driven by another teenager in 2006.

"We don't want to say that teens are a menace to us all, but the reality is, when teen drivers crash, it's people in other cars or teen passengers who end up dying," says Justin McNaull of the auto club AAA, which supports passenger limits to age 21 or even 25.

But Gregg D. Trautmann, an attorney and parent of two teens, believes some of the laws might actually be dangerous. He filed a suit against New Jersey three years ago, arguing that Kyleigh's Law **violates** federal driver privacy laws. He and other critics of the law also worry that marking a teen car may attract predators. The New Jersey Supreme

Drivers under age 21 are required to have a red decal on their license plate in New Jersey.

Court ruled against him this summer, but Trautmann says he plans to appeal to the US Supreme Court.

"We have young people flying Apache helicopters in Afghanistan to protect us; you're saying you can't drive a car past 11 [at night]?" says Trautmann.

For others, like Megan Lavery, a senior at Mainland Regional High School near Atlantic City, New Jersey, concerns about privacy need to be weighed against the dangers of teen driving. Megan often appears on local TV to remind students about a tragedy in 2011, when an SUV crowded with eight Mainland football players crashed, killing four of them. Now, more than a year later, she says, students have become more complacent about packing friends into their cars.

"Even I forget sometimes," she says. "You don't forget about what happened, but somebody asks you for a ride home, and you think, it's only a couple of blocks. It's easy to forget that the rules are there to keep us safe. A couple of blocks can change a whole life."

Pledging Against Distracted Driving

Eighteen percent of crashes that resulted in injuries in 2010 were related to distracted driving. At Distraction.gov, teens can sign a pledge like the one below, promising not only to drive phone-free, but to help others drive phone-free too.

TAKE **THE PLEDGE**

The fight to end distracted driving starts with you. Make the commitment to drive phone-free today.

Distracted driving kills and injures thousands of people each year. I pledge to:

- *Protect lives by never texting or talking on the phone while driving*
- *Be a good passenger and speak out if the driver in my car is distracted*
- *Encourage my friends and family to drive phone-free*

SIGNATURE: _____

DATE: _____

Source: Distraction.gov, 2013

CAN TEENS BE TRUSTED TO KNOW THEIR LIMIT WHEN IT COMES TO CREDIT?

4321 9876 5012 9900

Data File

Credit and debit cards, income, and savings are all part of money management. How does it all add up for teens?

What Do Teens Know About Money?

- According to a survey, 77% of teens think they are knowledgeable about how to manage money, including budgets, savings, and investments.
- 60% of teens say they know how to find the best deal when shopping for something, and 60% say they understand the difference between debit and **credit** cards.
- Only 35% say they know how to manage a **credit** card, 31% understand **credit** card **interest** and **fees**, and 31% can explain a **credit** score.
- 75% of teens say that learning more about **finances** is a top **priority**. 49% say they've learned about money management in school.

Saving and Spending

- 67% of teens have a job. The average **income** is $1,631 per year.
- 77% of teens call themselves "Super Savers" rather than "Big Spenders." The average savings is $966.
- 28% of teens owe money, with an average **debt** of $252.
- On average, teens spend $19 per week.

(Source: Charles Schwab & Co., 2011)

BUYER, BEWARE!

Before you apply for a credit card, know how to use this tool wisely—or pay a hefty price.

by Brooke Stephens

Wherever you look, MasterCard, Visa, American Express, and Discover logos invite you to shop with a **credit** card. TV commercials and the Internet show you how you can use a **credit** card to take a trip, get that new cell phone, download iTunes, or have dinner out after a movie at the mall with your buddies.

As a first-year college student at Norfolk State University in Virginia, Sanyika Galloway Boyce learned the hard way how easy it is to get into **credit** card **debt**. "Being one of seven children, money was always tight, and there was something sophisticated about other students who used **credit** cards to pay for almost everything," says Boyce. For six months, she ignored the **credit** card-company woman with the clipboard offering the free portable radio. But one stressful afternoon, Boyce stopped to chat. After a quick look at the simple application, she convinced herself that it was okay to have a $500-limit **credit** card for emergencies.

"When my boyfriend's car broke down, that emergency cost $256, and soon a new outfit for a holiday party, movie tickets, and dinners out on weekends also became 'emergencies,'" Boyce admits. "And it felt great to be signing my name on the charge receipt."

About a third of high school seniors say they use credit cards.

Within a year, that one **credit** card was joined by four more, and Boyce owed more than $5,000. Every dime of the earnings from her part-time job was going to make small payments that left her broke. As she learned, shopping and charging when you don't have the cash leads to an agonizing nightmare of **financial** chaos.

> ## "If you can eat it, drink it, or wear it, pay cash or don't buy it."

THE HISTORY OF CREDIT CARDS

Credit cards were created in 1950 for businesspeople to pay for plane tickets, hotels, and meals when traveling. Each month, they paid the full amount owed and had one receipt for all their expenses. Visa, introduced by Bank of America in 1964, allowed individual **credit** card holders to use extended monthly payments for large purchases, to be paid back with **interest**.

Paying with cash is "the best way to stay out of unnecessary **debt**," says P. J. Gunter, a **financial** counselor for My Money Matters of Houston. "If you can eat it, drink it, or wear it, pay cash or don't buy it." Still, not everyone can make every purchase with cash, and that's where **credit** can be a useful tool—if you use it well.

KNOW THE FACTS ABOUT CREDIT

Buying a home, purchasing a car, starting a business, and getting a student loan for college are smart uses of **credit**. But most of us use **credit** cards for other purposes, as Boyce did. Before you sign on the dotted line and get ready to start swiping the plastic, know these key facts about **credit** cards.

1. Credit is about borrowing. **Credit** is a temporary loan that must be repaid with **interest**. With a **credit** card, a bank makes a loan to you based on an agreement you sign promising to repay the loan. Each plastic card represents an amount, from $500 to $25,000, that the bank has decided to make available to you. You borrow that money for a limited period of time and repay it all at once or in a series of payments. Think of **credit** cards as a temporary replacement for cash.

2. Pay on time or pay **interest**. When the monthly statement comes in the mail, you are billed for the full amount due. If you don't have the money to cover the bill, you might opt to pay the **minimum** due, or a portion of the full amount. In this instance, you pay **interest** on the **balance** of your loan until you pay off your **debt**. You agree to those terms when you apply for a **credit** card.

The cost of paying over time can be expensive. For a student with little **income** and no track record for payments, the **interest** rate may be as high as 21 percent. That means that if you pay a **minimum** payment of $23 each month on a $1,000 **credit** card **balance** with a 21 percent **interest**

rate, it will take you 83 months (almost seven years) to repay the total due. The final cost will be $1,897—nearly twice the original amount borrowed.

Do you want to be paying for a Friday night dinner date five years from now, when it will cost you twice as much and you won't even remember whom you were with or what you ate? Probably not. Visit finance.youngmoney.com/ calculators_tools for more information about the long-term cost of paying the **minimum** amount due each month.

If you only make the minimum payments, paying off credit card debt will take longer and result in more fees.

Late payments can cost you, too. Gunter compares making late monthly payments to turning in your homework late. "Eventually, the news gets out about your 'poor behavior' to all of the banks, **credit** card companies, and department stores, and you will soon lose the privilege of using a **credit** card," Gunter says. "You will also have penalty costs in the form of extra **fees** of $25 to $50 per month added to your **debt**."

3. Credit card use earns a performance score. Points are also given (or taken away) based on how you perform with your **credit** card, the same way you score points or incur penalties in a basketball game. In the world of **credit**, it's called a **credit** score, and it ranges from 250 to 850. Students usually start with a mid-range score of 620 points, but that figure drops rapidly if you miss payments or make late payments.

Banks and **credit** card companies regularly grade and **evaluate** how you use your **credit** cards and how dependable you are at paying them back. "Graduating from high school and college may seem like the end of the 'getting good grades' process, but it isn't," says Barbara Emery, **financial** educator at the University of Delaware Center for Economic Education and

Entrepreneurship. "The focus changes from how you did on your history test to how you manage your bill paying, and [banks and **credit** card companies] rate your performance every 30 days."

> # Using a credit card wisely is the beginning of establishing a good reputation with money.

Three major national **credit** bureaus—Experian, TransUnion, and Equifax—collect and record all payment information, including where you live and work, when and how often you use your **credit** card, and whether you pay your **balance** in full or make regular monthly payments before the due date. That becomes your **credit** history, which stays in their files for seven years and is used by banks, student loan lenders, and insurance companies to **evaluate** your money management skills.

4. Poor **credit** has lifestyle consequences. An employer or a **potential** employer is able to check your **credit** report to see whether you manage money responsibly, particularly if the position requires you to handle money. (An employer cannot check your **credit** without your permission, however.) After college, when that first career move appears, the job opportunity of a lifetime may vanish if your **credit** report says you have too much **debt** or if you haven't paid your bills on time. The same goes for getting an apartment when you leave home. Landlords check **credit** reports to see your bill-paying habits; they want to know whether you will be late with the rent.

CREDIT CAN BE A GREAT TOOL

Credit works best when you understand how to manage it. Using a credit card wisely is the beginning of establishing a good reputation with money. One universal card, such as Visa or MasterCard, is more than enough because it is accepted almost everywhere and the **interest** rate is much lower than department store cards, which usually start at 21.9 percent **interest**. As Mark Twain said, "**Interest** is something that should be earned, not paid."

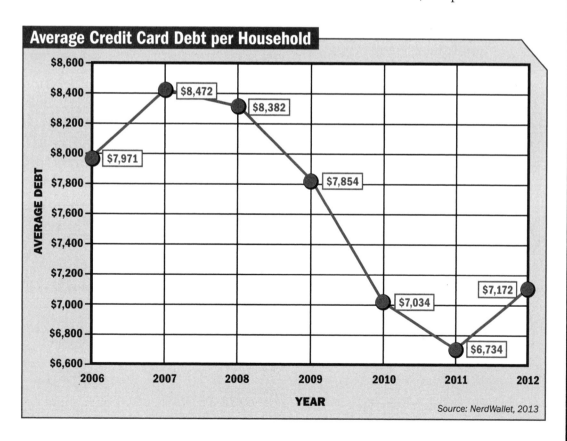

Average Credit Card Debt per Household

Source: NerdWallet, 2013

IF AT FIRST YOU DON'T SUCCEED

Common Mistakes Young Adults Make With Money and How to Avoid Them

Everybody makes mistakes with their money. The important thing is to keep them to a **minimum**. And one of the best ways to accomplish that is to learn from the mistakes of others. Here is our list of the top mistakes young people (and even many not-so-young people) make with their money, and what you can do to avoid these mistakes in the first place.

❶ BUYING ITEMS YOU DON'T NEED . . . AND PAYING EXTRA FOR THEM IN INTEREST

Every time you have an urge to do a little "impulse buying" and you use your **credit** card but you don't pay in full by the due date, you could be paying **interest** on that purchase for months or years to come. Spending money for something you really don't need can be a big waste of your money. But you can make the matter worse, a lot worse, by putting the purchase on a **credit** card and paying monthly **interest** charges.

Research major purchases and comparison shop before you buy. Ask yourself if you really need the item. Even better, wait a day or two, or just a few hours, to think things over rather than making a quick and costly decision you may come to regret.

There are good reasons to pay for major purchases with a **credit** card, such as extra protections if you have problems with the items. But if you charge a purchase with a **credit** card instead of paying by cash, check, or debit card (which automatically deducts the money from your bank account), be smart about how you repay. For example, take advantage of offers of "zero-percent interest" on **credit** card purchases for a certain number of months (but understand when and how **interest** charges could begin).

And, pay the entire **balance** on your **credit** card or as much as you can to avoid or **minimize** **interest** charges, which can add up **significantly**.

"If you pay only the **minimum** amount due on your **credit** card, you may end up paying more in **interest** charges than what the item cost you to begin with," said Janet Kincaid, FDIC senior consumer affairs officer. Example: If you pay only the **minimum** payment due on a $1,000 computer, let's say it's about $20 a month, your total cost at an Annual Percentage Rate of more than 18 percent can be close to $3,000, and it will take you nearly 19 years to pay it off.

GETTING TOO DEEPLY IN DEBT

Being able to borrow allows us to buy clothes or computers, take a vacation, or purchase a home or a car. But taking on too much **debt** can be a problem, and each year millions of adults of all ages find themselves struggling to pay their loans, **credit** cards, and other bills.

Learn to be a good money manager by following the basic strategies in this special report. Also recognize the warning signs of a serious **debt** problem. These may include borrowing money to make payments on loans you already have, deliberately paying bills late, and putting off doctor visits or other important activities because you think you don't have enough money.

If you get into trouble with debt, pay off your balances with the highest interest rates first.

If you believe you're experiencing **debt** overload, take corrective measures. For example, try to pay off your highest **interest**-rate loans (usually your **credit** cards) as soon as possible, even if you have higher **balances** on other loans. For new purchases, instead of using your **credit** card, try paying with cash, a check, or a debit card.

"There are also reliable **credit** counselors you can turn to for help at little or no cost," added Rita Wiles Ross, an FDIC attorney. "Unfortunately, you also need to be aware that there are scams masquerading as 'credit repair clinics' and other companies, such as 'debt consolidators,' that may charge big fees for unfulfilled promises or services you can perform on your own."

> Pay the entire balance on your credit card or as much as you can to avoid or minimize interest charges.

For more guidance on how to get out of debt safely or find a reputable credit counselor, start at the Federal Trade Commission (FTC) website at www.consumer.ftc.gov/topics/dealing-debt.

PAYING BILLS LATE OR OTHERWISE TARNISHING YOUR REPUTATION

Companies called credit bureaus prepare credit reports for use by lenders, employers, insurance companies, landlords, and others who need to know someone's financial reliability, based largely on each person's track record paying bills and debts. Credit bureaus, lenders, and other companies also produce "credit scores" that attempt to summarize and evaluate a person's credit record using a point system.

While one or two late payments on your loans or other regular commitments (such as rent or phone bills) over a long period may not seriously damage your credit record, making a habit of it will count against you. Over time you could be charged a higher interest rate on your credit card or a loan that you really want and need. You could be turned down for a job or an apartment. It could cost you extra when you apply for auto insurance. Your credit record will also be damaged by a bankruptcy filing or a court order to pay money as a result of a lawsuit.

So, pay your monthly bills on time. Also, periodically review your credit reports from the nation's three major credit bureaus—Equifax, Experian, and TransUnion—to make sure their information accurately reflects the accounts you have and your payment history, especially if you intend to apply for credit for something important in the near future. For information about your rights to obtain free copies of

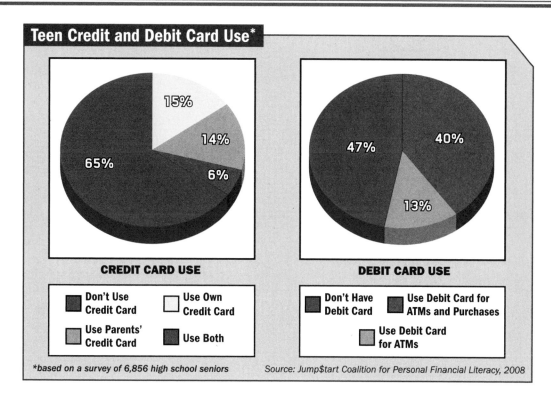

Teen Credit and Debit Card Use*

CREDIT CARD USE

15%
14%
65%
6%

DEBIT CARD USE

47%
40%
13%

Legend (Credit Card Use):
- Don't Use Credit Card
- Use Own Credit Card
- Use Parents' Credit Card
- Use Both

Legend (Debit Card Use):
- Don't Have Debit Card
- Use Debit Card for ATMs and Purchases
- Use Debit Card for ATMs

*based on a survey of 6,856 high school seniors

Source: Jump$tart Coalition for Personal Financial Literacy, 2008

your **credit** report and have errors corrected, see the FTC's fact sheet "Free Credit Reports" online at www.consumer.ftc.gov/articles/0155-free-credit-reports.

❷ HAVING TOO MANY CREDIT CARDS

Two to four cards (including any from department stores, oil companies, and other retailers) is the right number for most adults. Why not more cards?

The more **credit** cards you carry, the more inclined you may be to use them for costly impulse buying. In addition, each card you own—even the ones you don't use—represents money

that you could borrow up to the card's spending limit. If you apply for new **credit** you will be seen as someone who, in theory, could get much deeper in **debt** and you may only qualify for a smaller or costlier loan.

Also be aware that card companies aggressively market their products on college campuses, at concerts, ball games, or other events often attended by young adults. Their offers may seem tempting and even harmless— perhaps a free T-shirt or Frisbee, or 10 percent off your first purchase if you just fill out an application for a new card—but you've got to consider the possible consequences we've just described. "Don't sign up for a

credit card just to get a great looking T-shirt," Kincaid added. "You may be better off buying that shirt at the store for $14.95 and saving yourself the **potential** costs and troubles from that extra card."

NOT WATCHING YOUR EXPENSES

It's very easy to overspend in some areas and take away from other **priorities**, including your long-term savings. Our suggestion is to try any system—ranging from a computer-based budget program to hand-written notes—that will help you keep track of your spending each month and enable you to set and stick to limits you consider appropriate. "A budget doesn't have to be complicated, intimidating or painful—just something that works for you in getting a handle on your spending," said Kincaid.

> "A budget doesn't have to be complicated, intimidating or painful—just something that works for you in getting a handle on your spending."

Want some specific ideas for ways to cut back on spending? A good place to start is the "66 Ways to Save Money" campaign.

NOT SAVING FOR YOUR FUTURE

We know it can be tough to scrape together enough money to pay for a place to live, a car, and other expenses each month. But experts say it's also important for young people to save money for their long-term goals, too, including perhaps buying a home, owning a business, or saving

Credit card companies offer promotions on many college campuses.

How Savings Grows Over Time*

AMOUNT SAVED: $3,500 — $3,000 — $2,500 — $2,000 — $1,500 — $1,000 — $500 — $50

$3,333
$1,042
$714

YEAR 1   YEAR 2   YEAR 3   YEAR 4   YEAR 5

YEARS

*3.5% interest rate compounded monthly for five years, initial deposit $50

⬤ $50 Monthly   ⬤ $15 Monthly   ⬤ $10 Monthly

Source: Federal Deposit Insurance Corporation, 2006

for your retirement (even though it may be 40 or 50 years away).

Start by "paying yourself first." That means even before you pay your bills each month you should put money into savings for your future. Often the simplest way is to arrange with your bank or employer to automatically transfer a certain amount each month to a savings account or to purchase a US Savings Bond or an investment, such as a mutual fund that buys stocks and bonds.

Even if you start with just $25 or $50 a month you'll be **significantly** closer to your goal. "The important thing is to start saving as early as you can—even saving for your retirement when that seems light-years away— so you can benefit from the effect of compound **interest**," said Donna Gambrell, a deputy director of the FDIC's Division of Supervision and Consumer Protection. Compound **interest** refers to when an investment earns **interest**, and later that combined amount earns more

NEW ACCOUNTS

Setting up automatic transfers into a savings account is an easy way to begin saving.

interest, and on and on until a much larger sum of money is the result after many years.

Banking institutions pay **interest** on savings accounts that they offer. However, bank deposits aren't the only way to make your money grow. "Investments, which include stocks, bonds, and mutual funds, can be attractive alternatives to bank deposits because they often provide a higher rate of return over long periods, but remember that there is the **potential** for a temporary or permanent loss in value," said James Williams, an FDIC consumer affairs specialist. "Young people especially should do their research and consider getting

professional advice before putting money into investments."

❸ PAYING TOO MUCH IN FEES

Whenever possible, use your own **financial** institution's automated teller machines or the ATMs owned by **financial** institutions that don't charge **fees** to non-customers. You can pay $1 to $4 in **fees** if you get cash from an ATM that isn't owned by your **financial** institution or isn't part of an ATM "network" that your bank belongs to. For more about how to save on ATM **fees**, see the tips from FDIC Consumer News online at www.fdic.gov/consumers/consumer/news/cnspr04/simple.html.

Try not to "bounce" checks—that is, writing checks for more money than you have in your account, which can trigger **fees** from your financial institution (about $15 to $30 for each check) and from merchants. The best precaution is to keep your checkbook up to date and closely monitor your balance, which is easier to do with online and telephone banking. Remember to record your debit card transactions from ATMs and merchants so that you will be sure to have enough money in your account when those withdrawals are processed by your bank.

Financial institutions also offer "overdraft protection" services that can help you avoid the embarrassment and inconvenience of having a check returned to a merchant. But be careful before signing up because these programs come with their own costs. Pay off your **credit** card **balance** each month, if possible, so you can avoid or minimize **interest** charges. Also send in your payment on time to avoid additional fees. If you don't expect to pay your **credit** card bill in full most months, consider using a card with a low **interest** rate and a generous "grace period" (the number of days before the card company starts charging you **interest** on new purchases).

NOT TAKING RESPONSIBILITY FOR YOUR FINANCES

Do a little comparison shopping to find accounts that match your needs at the right cost. Be sure to review your bills and bank statements as soon as possible after they arrive or monitor your accounts **periodically** online or by telephone. You want to make sure there are no errors, unauthorized charges, or **indications** that a thief is using your identity to commit fraud.

Keep copies of any contracts or other documents that describe your bank accounts, so you can refer to

them in a dispute. Also remember that the quickest way to fix a problem usually is to work directly with your bank or other service provider.

> ## Be sure to review your bills and bank statements as soon as possible after they arrive or monitor your accounts periodically online or by telephone.

"Many young people don't take the time to check their receipts or make the necessary phone calls or write letters to correct a problem," one banker told *FDIC Consumer News.* "Resolving these issues can be time consuming and exhausting but doing so can add up to hundreds of dollars."

FINAL THOUGHTS

Even if you are fortunate enough to have parents or other loved ones you can turn to for help or advice as you start handling money on your own, it's really up to you to take charge of your **finances**. Doing so can be intimidating for anyone. It's easy to become overwhelmed or frustrated. And everyone makes mistakes. The important thing is to take action.

Start small if you need to. Stretch to pay an extra $50 a month on your **credit** card bill or other **debts**. Find two or three ways to cut your spending. Put an extra $50 a month into a savings account. Even little changes can add up to big savings over time.

Also remember that being **financially** independent doesn't mean you're entirely on your own. There are always government agencies, including the FDIC and other organizations that can help with your questions or problems.

Sample Credit Card Statement

New balance	$3,000.00
Minimum payment due	$90.00
Payment due date	4/20/12

Late Payment Warning: If we do not receive your minimum payment by the date listed above, you may have to pay a $35 late fee and your APRs may be increased up to the Penalty APR of 28.99%.

Minimum Payment Warning: If you make only the minimum payment each period, you will pay more in interest and it will take you longer to pay off your balance. For example:

If you make no additional charges using this card and each month you pay...	You will pay off the balance shown on this statement in about...	And you will end up paying an estimated total of...
Only the minimum payment	11 years	$4,745
$103	3 years	$3,712 (Savings = $1,033)

Source: Federal Reserve, 2010

BANKRUPT BY 25

People under age 25 make up the fastest-growing age group filing for bankruptcy. Easy credit, bigger student loans, and financial illiteracy are fueling the trend.

by Dirk Smillie

Vivienne Decker, an 18-year-old freshman at the University of South Carolina, doesn't have a **credit** card and doesn't want one, for now anyway. "I'm a shopaholic and I know I can't trust myself," she says.

> In 2001, 150,000 people under 25 filed for bankruptcy.

But Decker isn't surprised to hear that she's part of the fastest-growing segment of the population seeking **bankruptcy** protection. She learned a lesson from her 21-year-old brother, Pip, who racked up $3,000 on his cards, charging everything from travel expenses to fraternity **fees**. It took him a year of part-time and full-time jobs to pay it off. "Right now," she says, "I do everything with cash."

For many teens, freshman year of college is the first time they have real control over their **finances**. Often, that means signing up for their first **credit** card. (You must be 18 to own one.)

ARE CREDIT CARDS TO BLAME?

But many find that it takes only a year or two for their newfound **financial** freedom to turn into a big liability. In 2001, 150,000 people under 25 filed for **bankruptcy**, a 150 percent increase over 1991. (**Bankruptcies** increased 58 percent for the population as a whole over the same period.)

While **bankruptcy** laws allow people in **financial** trouble to eliminate or **restructure** their **debt**, filing for **bankruptcy** is not a panacea: it can stain your **credit** history for 10 years.

Some experts say part of what's fueling the **bankruptcy** boom is more aggressive marketing to young people by **credit**-card companies. They "target high school and college-age people because they see them as the only growth opportunities in a saturated market," says Elizabeth Warren, a Harvard law professor and **bankruptcy** expert.

> **Only nine states require students to complete a course that covers personal finance in high school.**

A good example is Decker's school, where no fewer than 15 **credit**-card vendors are **promoting** cards. Free T-shirts, movie tickets, coolers, and shopping coupons are used as enticements. Some schools offer cards with university logos; others charge card companies for the privilege of setting up sales tables on campus.

Credit-card companies say it's simplistic to blame them for the **bankruptcy** boom among young people. "There are a lot of factors behind **bankruptcies**," says Catherine Cummings, vice president of consumer affairs at MasterCard, who notes that most students pay off their bills.

Indeed, experts say mushrooming college costs are a major culprit. The cost of attending four-year universities has climbed 66 percent over the past decade. By the time the average college student graduates, he or she has an average of $19,000 in **debt** (compared with $11,400 five years ago), according to student-loan provider Nellie Mae. The Senate Banking Committee reports that 73 percent of college freshmen used student-loan money to pay off **debt**, notably **credit**-card **balances**.

LEARNING TO MANAGE CREDIT

The key is to limit the **debt** you take on, says Joline Godfrey, chief executive of Independent Means,

The average college graduate has $19,000 in debt.

which provides **financial** education for those ages 5–25. To do that, she advises, "Own just one **credit** card." And she says young people should learn how to manage their money early on.

But for many teens, **financial** literacy isn't exactly a hot topic. Only nine states require students to complete a course that covers personal **finance** in high school, according to surveys of state education standards.

Some colleges now realize that students are arriving on campus without the skills they need to manage their **finances**. While the University of South Carolina welcomes card vendors to campus, it also offers classes like University 101, an introduction to campus life, which includes visits by bank representatives who offer tips on using **credit** wisely and encourage students not to run up high **credit**-card **balances**.

There are also several nonprofit organizations that provide **financial** literacy tools for young people, including Consumer Jungle (www.consumerjungle.com) and Jumpstart Coalition for Personal Financial Literacy (www.jumpstart.org).

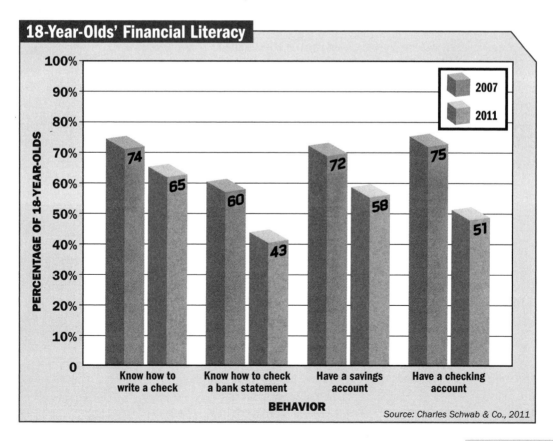

18-Year-Olds' Financial Literacy

Legend: 2007, 2011

PERCENTAGE OF 18-YEAR-OLDS

- Know how to write a check: 74, 65
- Know how to check a bank statement: 60, 43
- Have a savings account: 72, 58
- Have a checking account: 75, 51

BEHAVIOR

Source: Charles Schwab & Co., 2011

Debate

When it comes to school, should teens plug in or opt out?

Data File

It's the school of the future: just log in to your computer and sign in to first period class! But do online classes really work?

A Boom in Online Learning

- The number of K–12 students enrolled full-time in online public school has increased 450% over the past five years, from 50,000 students in 2006–2007 to 275,000 students in 2011–2012.
- During the 2011–2012 school year, it is estimated that over 2,500,000 K–12 students took at least one online course.
- Thirty-one states and Washington DC have statewide, full-time online schools.

(Source: Evergreen Education Group, 2012)

Increasing Internet Access

- As of 2010, more than 68% of US households have Internet **access**, and over 77% have a computer, making it easier for students to get online for school.

(Source: International Association for K–12 Online Learning, 2013)

Keeping Costs Down

- The average annual cost to educate a student online is $6,400, compared to an average cost of $11,282 per student at a traditional school. That's a savings of nearly $5,000 per student every year!

(Source: International Association for K–12 Online Learning, 2012)

Cyber Students

Should students be required to take online courses?

by Adele Birkenes and Dontaé Brown

Stash your pencils, pens, and notebooks. Students across the country are making the grade without ever setting foot inside a classroom with online courses. Most middle schools and high schools that offer online classes do not require students to take them. But four states require high school students to pass at least one online course to graduate—Michigan, Florida, Alabama, and Idaho. Starting in 2012, Idaho will require all incoming high school freshmen to pass two such courses to graduate, making it the first state to require two online credits. [Editor's update: In November 2012, this legislation was repealed.]

Supporters of the laws say that online classes help prepare students for the **digital** world. Proponents also argue that online classes can save school districts money by allowing students to take classes from home and **accommodating** larger class sizes. Critics of the requirements argue that they may harm some students' educations. They worry that the online classes do not serve the needs of the students who need **individualized** attention.

Should students be required to take online courses? *Current Events* student reporters Adele Birkenes and Dontaé Brown each keyed in a side.

With online learning, students miss out on face-to-face interactions with their peers and teachers.

Log On

Most students are adept at playing computer games, social networking, emailing, and doing homework on the computer. So why not have them spend some of that time getting credit for a class? A recent survey published by the Sloan Consortium showed that 31 percent of students in college take at least one course online. If students are required to take online courses to graduate, they will have an easier time adjusting to college and the workplace.

Online courses also enrich the learning experience. Christina Field, a teacher from Greenbelt, Maryland, agrees. "Online courses open up a student to a variety of resources that they might not have available in the classroom," she says. Those resources, such as **interactive** lessons and videos, will make classes more fun and **effective**.

Finally, online courses can be **accessed** anywhere at any time as long as there is an Internet connection. Students who are traveling or in the hospital will not be left behind. In addition, students in rural areas and small towns will have the same academic opportunities as students in cities, and online courses will let students set their own pace.
—**Adele Birkenes**

Power Down

Students should not be **mandated** to take online classes in order to complete high school. Yes, students already spend a great deal of time online, but they spend that time chatting with their friends, playing computer games, and using social networks. How does anyone expect

Taking online courses in high school helps prepare students for college, where online courses are the norm.

students to curtail their online activities and use online time to earn school credits?

I understand that online classes are a norm on college campuses, but we are still kids. School is the place where we learn to **interact** with one another. School is where we learn to hold meaningful discussions and to read one another's body language and facial expressions. Online classes defeat that purpose.

With online classes, students might be less **inclined** to seek help from a teacher or other real life source. Students could more easily hide their lack of understanding. Online classes' lack of close contact would not help struggling students. NaReida Crandall, a college counselor in New York City, agrees. "Online classes take a great deal of **discipline** and focus," she says. "Many high school students have not developed the skill set necessary to be successful in this type of learning." —**Dontaé Brown**

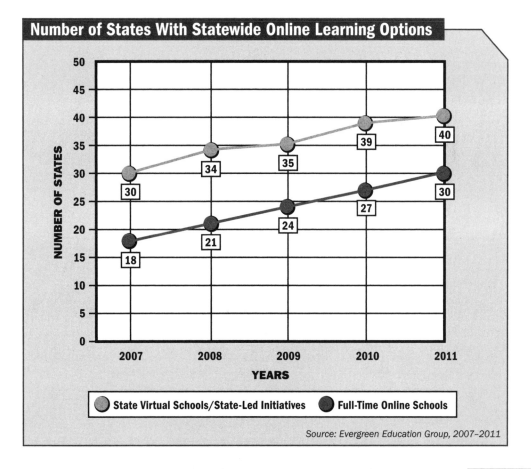

Number of States With Statewide Online Learning Options

State Virtual Schools/State-Led Initiatives — 30, 34, 35, 39, 40

Full-Time Online Schools — 18, 21, 24, 27, 30

NUMBER OF STATES / YEARS (2007, 2008, 2009, 2010, 2011)

Source: Evergreen Education Group, 2007–2011

More Pupils Are Learning Online, Fueling Debate on Quality

by Trip Gabriel

MEMPHIS–Jack London was the subject in Daterrius Hamilton's online English 3 course. In a high school classroom packed with computers, he read a brief biography of London with single-paragraph excerpts from the author's works. But the curriculum did not require him, as it had generations of English students, to wade through a tattered copy of *The Call of the Wild* or "To Build a Fire."

In Memphis, every student must take an online course to graduate.

Mr. Hamilton, who had failed English 3 in a **conventional** classroom and was hoping to earn credit online to graduate, was asked a question about the meaning of social Darwinism. He pasted the question into Google and read a summary of a Wikipedia entry. He copied the language, spell-checked it, and emailed it to his teacher.

> ## Critics say online education is really driven by a desire to spend less on teachers and buildings.

Mr. Hamilton, 18, is among the expanding ranks of students in kindergarten through Grade 12—more than one million in the United States, by one **estimate**—taking online courses.

Advocates of such courses say they allow schools to offer not only makeup courses, the fastest-growing area, but also a richer menu of electives and Advanced Placement classes when there are not enough students to fill a classroom.

But critics say online education is really driven by a desire to spend less on teachers and buildings, especially as state and local budget crises force deep cuts to education. They note that there is no sound research showing that online courses at the K–12 level are **comparable** to face-to-face learning.

❶ Here in Memphis, in one of the most ambitious online programs of its kind, every student must take an online course to graduate, beginning with current sophomores. Some study online versions of courses taught in classrooms in the same building. Officials for Memphis City Schools say they want to give students skills they will need in college, where online courses are increasingly common, and in the 21st-century workplace.

But it is also true that Memphis is spending only $164 for each student in an online course. Administrators say they have never calculated an apples-to-apples comparison for the cost of online versus in-person education, but around the country skeptics say online courses are a stealthy way to cut corners.

"It's a cheap education, not because it benefits the students," said Karen Aronowitz, president of the teachers' union in Miami, where 7,000 high school students were assigned to study online in computer labs this year because there were not enough teachers to comply with state class-size caps.

"This is being proposed for even your youngest students," Ms. Aronowitz said. "Because it's good for the kids? No. This is all about cheap."

In Idaho, the state superintendent of education plans to push a requirement that high school students take four or more online courses, following a bill that passed the Legislature last week to provide every student with a laptop, paid for from a state fund for educators' salaries.

Chicago and New York City have introduced pilot online learning programs. In New York, Innovation Zone, or iZone, includes online makeup and Advanced Placement courses at 30 high schools, as well as personalized after-school computer drills in math and English for elementary students.

Reza Namin, superintendent of schools in Westbrook, Maine, which faces a $6.5 million budget deficit,

said he could not justify continuing to pay a Chinese-language teacher for only 10 interested students. But he was able to offer Chinese online through the Virtual High School Global Consortium, a nonprofit school based in Massachusetts.

> **Nationwide, an estimated 1.03 million students at the K–12 level took an online course in 2007–2008, up 47 percent from two years earlier.**

The **virtual** high school says its list of client schools has grown to 770, up 34 percent in two years, because of local budget cuts.

❷ Nationwide, an **estimated** 1.03 million students at the K–12 level took an online course in 2007–2008, up 47 percent from two years earlier, according to the Sloan Consortium, an advocacy group for online education. About 200,000 students

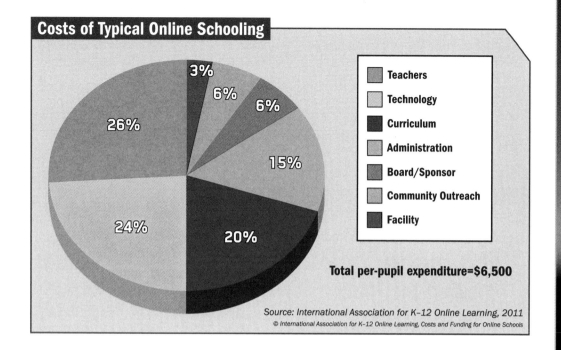

Costs of Typical Online Schooling

- 3%
- 6%
- 6%
- 26%
- 15%
- 24%
- 20%

Legend:
- Teachers
- Technology
- Curriculum
- Administration
- Board/Sponsor
- Community Outreach
- Facility

Total per-pupil expenditure=$6,500

Source: International Association for K–12 Online Learning, 2011
© International Association for K–12 Online Learning, Costs and Funding for Online Schools

attend online schools full time, often charter schools that appeal to home-schooling families, according to another report.

The growth has come despite a cautionary review of research by the United States Department of Education in 2009. It found benefits in online courses for college students, but it concluded that few rigorous studies had been done at the K–12 level, and policy makers "lack scientific evidence of the **effectiveness**" of online classes.

The fastest growth has been in makeup courses for students who failed a regular class. Advocates say the courses let students who were bored or left behind learn at their own pace.

But even some proponents of online classes are dubious about makeup courses, also known as credit recovery—or, derisively, click-click credits—which high schools, especially those in high-poverty districts, use to increase graduation rates and avoid federal sanctions.

"I think many people see online courses as being a way of being able to remove a pain point, and that is, how are they going to increase their graduation rate?" said Liz Pape, president of the Virtual High School Global Consortium. If credit recovery were working, she said, the need for

remedial classes in college would be declining—but the opposite is true.

In Memphis, Mr. Hamilton's school, Sheffield High, once qualified as a "dropout factory" with a graduation rate below 60 percent.

> ## "We can educate more students at a higher level with limited resources, and online technology and courses play a big part in that."

Now the class of 2011 is on target to graduate 86 percent of its students, said Elvin Bell, the school's "graduation coach," an increase **attributable** in part to a longer school day and online credit recovery.

Sixty-one students are in the courses this semester, including Mr. Hamilton, whose average in English 3 is below passing. Melony Smith, his online teacher, said she had not immediately recognized that his answer on the Jack London assignment was copied from the Web, but she said plagiarism was a problem for many students.

Students' strong desire to pass, she added, meant most were diligent about the work. "A lot of my students send me messages and say, 'I really need this class to graduate, and I will do anything; please call me because I don't understand something,'" Ms. Smith said.

The district has bought software for 54 online courses, including Algebra 1, biology and United States history, from the Florida Virtual School, a large state-run online school.

❸ Memphis supplies its own teachers, mostly classroom teachers who supplement their incomes by contracting to work 10 hours a week with 150 students online. That is one-fourth of the time they would devote to teaching the same students face to face.

But administrators insisted that their chief motive was to **enhance** student learning, not save money in a year when the 108,000-student district is braced for cuts of $100 million and hundreds of jobs.

"What the online environment does is continue to provide rich offerings and delivery systems to our students with these resource challenges," said Irving Hamer, the deputy superintendent.

Like other education debates, this one divides along ideological lines. K–12 online learning is championed by conservative-leaning policy groups that favor broadening school choice, including Jeb Bush's Foundation for Excellence in Education, which has called on states to provide all students with "Internet **access** devices" and remove bans on for-profit **virtual** schools.

Teachers' unions and others say much of the push for online courses, like vouchers and charter schools, is intended to channel taxpayers' money into the private sector.

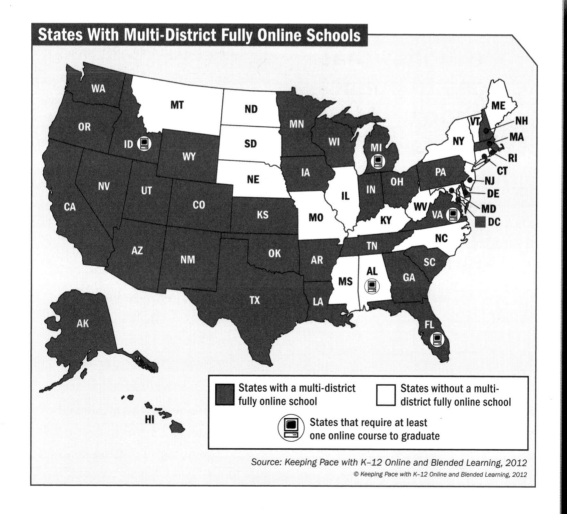

States With Multi-District Fully Online Schools

States with a multi-district fully online school

States without a multi-district fully online school

States that require at least one online course to graduate

Source: Keeping Pace with K–12 Online and Blended Learning, 2012

© Keeping Pace with K–12 Online and Blended Learning, 2012

"What they want is to substitute technology for teachers," said Alex Molnar, professor of education policy at Arizona State University.

In Idaho, Governor C. L. Otter and the elected superintendent of public instruction, Tom Luna, both Republicans, promoted giving students laptops and requiring online courses.

> "It's about getting a piece of the money that goes to public schools," Ms. Wood said. "The big corporations want to make money off the backs of our children."

The State Legislature, pressed by critics who said the online **mandate** would cost teachers jobs, rejected it, but Mr. Luna said in an interview that he would propose it this summer through the State Board of Education, which supports him.

"I have no doubt we'll get a robust rule through them," he said. Four online courses is "going to be the starting number."

Online courses are part of a package of sweeping changes, including merit pay and ending tenure, which Idaho lawmakers approved, that Mr. Luna said would improve education.

"We can educate more students at a higher level with limited resources, and online technology and courses play a big part in that," he said.

Sherri Wood, president of the Idaho Education Association, the teachers' union, strongly disagreed. She said Mr. Luna's 2010 re-election campaign had received more than $50,000 in contributions from online education companies like K–12 Inc., a Virginia-based operator of online charter schools that received $12.8 million from Idaho last year.

"It's about getting a piece of the money that goes to public schools," Ms. Wood said. "The big corporations want to make money off the backs of our children."

Mr. Luna replied that political contributors had never had an inside track in winning education contracts.

Ready Player One

by Ernest Cline

My avatar materialized in front of my locker on the second floor of my high school—the exact spot where I'd been standing when I'd logged out the night before.

I glanced up and down the hallway. My **virtual** surroundings looked almost (but not quite) real. Everything inside the OASIS was beautifully rendered in three dimensions. Unless you pulled focus and stopped to examine your surroundings more closely, it was easy to forget that everything you were seeing was computer-generated. And that was with my crappy school-issued OASIS console. I'd heard that if you **accessed** the simulation with a new state-of-the-art immersion rig, it was almost impossible to tell the OASIS from **reality**.

I touched my locker door and it popped open with a soft metallic click. The inside was sparsely decorated. A picture of Princess Leia posing with a blaster pistol. A group photo of the members of Monty Python in their Holy Grail costumes. James Halliday's *Time* magazine cover. I reached up and tapped the stack of textbooks on the locker's top shelf and they vanished, then reappeared in my avatar's item inventory.

Aside from my textbooks, my avatar had only a few meager possessions: a flashlight, and iron shortsword, a small bronze shield, and a suit of banded leather armor. These items were all nonmagical and of low quality, but they were the best I could afford. Items in the OASIS had just as much value as things in the real world (sometimes more), and you couldn't pay for them with food vouchers. The OASIS credit was the coin of the realm, and in these dark times, it was also one of the world's most stable currencies, valued higher than the dollar, pound, euro, or yen.

A small mirror was mounted inside my locker door, and I caught a glimpse of my **virtual** self as I closed it. I'd designed my avatar's face and body to look, more or less, like my own. My avatar had a slightly smaller nose than me, and he was taller. And thinner. And more muscular. And he didn't have any teenage acne. But aside from these minor details, we looked more or less identical. The school's strictly enforced dress code required that all student avatars be human, and of the same gender and age as the student. No giant hermaphrodite demon unicorn avatars were allowed. Not on school grounds, anyway.

> **Anonymity was one of the major perks of the OASIS. Inside the simulation, no one knew who you really were, unless you wanted them to.**

You could give your OASIS avatar any name you liked, as long as it was unique. Meaning you had to pick a name that hadn't already been taken by someone else. Your avatar's name was also your email address and chat ID, so you wanted it to be cool and easy to remember. Celebrities had been known to pay huge sums of money to buy an avatar name they wanted from a cyber-squatter who had already reserved it.

When I'd first created my OASIS account, I'd named my avatar Wade_the_Great. After that, I kept changing it every few months, usually to something equally ridiculous. But my avatar now had the same name for over five years. On the day the Hunt began, the day I'd decided to become a gunter, I'd renamed my avatar Parzival, after the knight of Arthurian legend who had found the Holy Grail. The other more common spellings of that knight's name, Perceval and Percival, had already been taken by other users. But I preferred the name Parzival, anyway. I thought it had a nice ring to it.

People rarely used their real names online. **Anonymity** was one of the major perks of the OASIS. Inside the simulation, no one knew who you really were, unless you wanted them to. Much of the OASIS's popularity and culture were built around this fact. Your real name, fingerprints, and retinal patterns were stored in your OASIS account, but Gregarious Simulation Systems kept that information encrypted and confidential. Even GSS's own employees couldn't look up an avatar's true identity. Back when Halliday was still running the company, GSS had won the right to keep every OASIS user's identity private in a landmark Supreme Court ruling.

When I'd first enrolled in the OASIS public school system, I was required to give them my real name, avatar name, mailing address, and Social Security number. That information was stored in my student profile, but only my principal had **access** to that. None of my teachers or fellow students knew who I really was, and vice versa.

Students weren't allowed to use their avatar names while they were at school. This was to prevent teachers from having to say ridiculous things like "Pimp_Grease, please pay attention!" Instead, students were required to use their real first names, followed by a number to **differentiate** them from other students with the same name. When I enrolled, there were already two other students at my school with the first name Wade, so I'd been assigned the student ID of Wade3. That name floated above my avatar's head whenever I was on school grounds.

> I didn't have the money to attend college, not even one in the OASIS, and my grades weren't good enough for a scholarship. My only plan after graduation was to become a full-time gunter.

The school bell rang and a warning flashed in the corner of my display, informing me that I had forty minutes until the start of first period. I began to walk my avatar down the hall, using a series of subtle hand motions to control its movements and actions. I could also use voice commands to move around, if my hands were otherwise occupied.

I strolled in the direction of World History classroom, smiling and waving to the familiar faces I passed. I was going to miss this place when I graduated in a few months. I wasn't looking forward to leaving school. I didn't have the money to attend college, not even one in the OASIS, and my grades weren't good enough for a scholarship. My only plan after graduation was to become a full-time gunter. I didn't have much choice. Winning the contest was my one chance of escaping the stacks. Unless I wanted to sign a five-year indenturement contract with some corporation, and that was about as appealing to me as rolling around in broken glass in my birthday suit.

As I continued down the hallway, other students began to materialize in front of their lockers, ghostly apparitions that rapidly solidified. The sound of chattering teenagers began to echo up and down the corridor. Before long, I heard an insult hurled in my direction.

"Hey, hey! If isn't Wade Three!" I heard a voice shout. I turned and saw Todd13, an obnoxious avatar I recognized from my Algebra II class. He was standing with several of his friends. "Great outfit, slick," he said. "Where did you snag the sweet threads?"

My avatar was wearing a black T-shirt and blue jeans, one of the default skins you could select when you created your account. Like his Cro-Magnon friends, Todd13 wore an expensive designer skin, probably purchased in some off-world mall.

> **Online, I didn't have a problem talking to people or making friends. But in the real world, interacting with other people— especially kids my own age— made me a nervous wreck.**

"Your mom bought them for me," I retorted without breaking my stride. "Tell her I said thanks, the next time you stop home to breast-feed and pick up your allowance." Childish, I know. But **virtual** or not, this was still high school—the most childish an insult, the more **effective** it was.

My jab elicited laughter from a few of his friends and some other students standing nearby. Todd13 scowled and his face actually turned red—a sign that he hadn't bothered to turn off his account's real-time emotion feature, which made your avatar mirror your facial expressions and body language. He was about to reply, but I muted him first, so I didn't hear what he said. I just smiled and continued on my way.

The ability to mute my peers was one of my favorite things about attending school online, and I took advantage of it almost daily. The best thing about it was that they could see that you'd muted them, and they couldn't do a damn thing about it. There was never any fighting on school grounds. The simulation simply didn't allow it. The entire planet of Ludus was a no-PvP zone, meaning no player-versus-player combat was permitted. At this school, the only real weapons were words, so I'd become skilled at wielding them.

★ ★ ★

I'd attended school in the real world up until the sixth grade. It hadn't been a very pleasant experience. I was a painfully shy, awkward kid, with low self-esteem and almost no social skills—a side effect of spending most of my childhood inside the OASIS. Online, I didn't have a problem talking to people or making friends. But in the real world, **interacting** with other people—especially kids my own age—made me a nervous wreck. I never knew how to act or what to say, and when I did work up the courage to speak, I always seemed to say the wrong thing.

> # Best of all, in the OASIS, no one could tell that I was fat, that I had acne, or that I wore the same shabby clothes every week.

My appearance was part of the problem. I was overweight, and had been for as long as I could remember. My bankrupt diet of government-subsidized sugar-and-starch-laden food was a **contributing** factor, but I was also an OASIS addict, so the only exercise I usually got back then was running away from bullies before and after school. To make matters worse, my limited wardrobe consisted entirely of ill-fitting clothes from thrift stores and donation bins—the social equivalent of having a bull's-eye painted on my forehead.

Even so, I tried my best to fit in. Year after year, my eyes would scan the lunchroom like a T-1000, searching for a clique that might accept me. But even the other outcasts wanted nothing to do with me. I was too weird, even for the weirdos. And girls? Talking to girls was out of the question. To me, they were like some exotic alien species, both beautiful and terrifying. Whenever I got near one of them, I invariably broke out in a cold sweat and lost the ability to speak in complete sentences.

For me, school had been a Darwinian exercise. A daily gauntlet of ridicule, abuse, and isolation. By the time I entered sixth grade, I was beginning to wonder if I'd be able to maintain my sanity until graduation, still six long years away.

Then, one glorious morning, our principal announced that any student with a passing grade-point average could apply for a transfer to the new OASIS public school system. The real public school system, the one run by the government, had been an underfunded, overcrowded train wreck for decades. And now the conditions at many schools had gotten so terrible that every kid with half a brain was being encouraged to stay at home and attend school online. I nearly broke my neck sprinting to the school office to submit my application. It was accepted, and I transferred to OASIS Public School #1873 the following semester.

Prior to my transfer, my OASIS avatar had never left the Incipio, the planet at the center of Sector One where new avatars were spawned at the time of their creation. There wasn't much to do on Incipio except chat with other noobs or shop in one of the giant **virtual** malls that covered the planet. If you wanted to go somewhere more interesting, you had to pay a teleportation fare to get there, and that cost money, something I didn't have. So my avatar was stranded on Incipio. That is, until my new school emailed me a teleportation voucher to cover the cost of my avatar's transport to Ludus, the planet where all of the OASIS public schools were located.

There were hundreds of school campuses here on Ludus, spread out evenly across the planet's surface. The schools were all identical, because the same construction code was copied and pasted in to a different location whenever a new school was needed. And since the buildings were just pieces of software, their design wasn't limited by monetary constraints, or even by the laws of physics. So every school was a grand palace of learning, with polished marble hallways, cathedral-like classrooms, zero-g gymnasiums, and **virtual** libraries containing every "school board approved" book ever written. On my first day at OPS #1873, I thought I'd died and gone to heaven. Now, instead of running a gauntlet of bullies and drug addicts on my walk to school each morning, I went straight to my hideout and stayed there all day. Best of all, in the OASIS, no one could tell that I was fat, that I had acne, or that I wore the same shabby clothes every week. Bullies couldn't pelt me with spitballs, give me atomic wedgies, or pummel me by the bike rack after school. No one could even touch me. In here, I was safe.

Meet the Author

ERNEST CLINE

Born: 1972 in Ashland, Ohio

Where Is He Now? Ernest lives with his wife and daughter in Austin, Texas.

Books: *Ready Player One* is Ernest's first novel. He also wrote the screenplay for the movie *Fanboys*, which was produced in 2009.

On the Future of the Internet: "Right now, we access the online world through our computer monitors and smartphone screens, but I think it's only a matter of time until the Internet evolves into an immersive virtual space that allows you to access all of your other data from inside it. Once the technology is there, instead of text-based chatrooms, we could have actual VR chatrooms that people can access with avatars, so it would be like you were actually hanging out in a room with other people, even though those other people might be spread all over the world. Once the people of planet Earth are all hanging out together online in a virtual world without any borders, I think it could change social networking, entertainment, and even politics."

Debate

ARE TEENS READY TO GET TO WORK?

Data File

High school graduates are more likely to be employed and tend to earn more money. But are high schools doing enough to prepare students for college and work?

Reflecting on High School

- Looking back one year later, 41% of graduates said they were "very satisfied" with their high school experience. Another 41% said they were "somewhat satisfied."

- 80% of graduates said they would change parts of their experience. 44% would take different classes.

- 66% said their schools did a good job of **preparing** them for college, but 33% said they should have done better. 58% said their schools did a good job of **preparing** them for work, but 41% said they should have done better.

(Source: Hart Research Associates, 2011)

What Employers Want

A survey showed that employers most value these skills:

- Being a team player (71%)
- **Focusing** on satisfying customers (68%)
- Motivating others (65%)
- Achieving critical objectives (62%)
- Working smart (60%)
- Working hard (57%)

(Source: OI Partners, 2012)

High School Classes, Take Two

- Remedial courses to reteach college students what they were expected to learn in high school cost an estimated $5.6 billion in 2007–08.

- About one in three college students need to take at least one remedial course. These students are only about half as likely to graduate college.

- Four out of five students taking remedial courses had high school GPAs above 3.0.

(Source: Alliance for Excellent Education, 2011)

Look to the Future

Even though planning a career can feel futile when so many people are losing jobs, experts say you should keep thinking about tomorrow.

by Betsy O'Donovan

From the president of the United States to the person picking up litter on the side of the road, more than 140 million people in the United States had jobs in the summer of 2009.

The bad news: that's 14.5 million fewer jobs than in the summer of 2008.

The good news: the U.S. Bureau of Labor Statistics projects that there will be 5-6 million more jobs by the year 2016. That's something students who are getting ready to enter the workforce can look forward to.

Career World was curious about what students can do to plan for those future jobs—some of which "haven't even been imagined yet," according to Marilyn Fettner, a career development counselor in Chicago.

"There are careers today that didn't exist five years ago," Fettner says. "An example of that is social network consultant." It's true: people get paid to spend their days on Twitter and Facebook, answering questions, making connections, and representing clients such as athletes and airlines.

Experts suggest that you start planning your career even before high school.

In fact, career **experts** say that the right **preparation** can put a fulfilling and fun career within everyone's grasp. How can you **prepare**? *Career World* turned to some **experts** for advice.

When should students start planning their careers?

"As they're leaving junior high school, and even before," says Julie Cruz, coordinator for the Einstein Enrichment Program at the Albert Einstein College of Medicine in New York. Cruz works to **prepare** high school students for careers

Counselors can help students identify their career interests.

in medicine and **focuses** on low-income and minority students, who make up only four percent of medical school applicants.

Cruz says the students she works with "are not getting the course work in high school that will get them into colleges that will get them into medical school," she said. "It's the domino **principle**."

That **principle** is true for all students, not just those **focused** on graduate or **professional** degrees, she says. Even having some idea of what **field** you might like to be in after high school will help you select the courses, activities, **mentors**, and internships that can help you reach your goals.

"It's like planning vacation," Cruz says. "If you don't know where you're going, you don't know what to pack."

Cruz adds that students should start imagining possible futures early, though many students do the groundwork for career planning without even realizing it.

"Your career's not only what you do for a living, but who you are," Cruz says. She suggests **focusing** on your greatest interests, which can be turned into skills and can, in turn, lead to a fulfilling career.

How can students get started in career planning?

"One of the most common things that people ask for first in approaching a career counselor is, 'Can you give me one of those tests that tell me what I can be?'" says Cynthia Kivland, who owns a career consulting company in Chicago and is the author of *From Smart to Smarter*, a book about career change and happiness at work. "That's a good place to start."

> ***"There are careers today that didn't exist five years ago."***

A lot of those tests are easy to find online, Kivland says. School counselors often have access to career interest tests that they like to use with students too. Students can review the results with their school counselors, who can help them figure out the next steps.

"We look at subject areas that people are attracted to, the kind of people they like to hang around with, the books they read, movies they like to watch, the websites they visit," Kivland told *Career World*. "All are clues to an interest pattern. After interests, we look at grades, at course work that you do well in. Your interest acts like a magnet for things that you're attracted to, and you tend to do well in that area."

Is it possible for students to try out a career to see whether it's a good fit?

Getting real experience in a **field** can be a useful window to the future. You'll get a better idea of what the trends are in a **field** and where you might fit in. That is where high school students have an advantage, Fettner notes, because students have time to research, job shadow, and ask for informational interviews that can help them see what their dream jobs are really like.

Fettner says that students should be bold when seeking **mentors** and information. Adults with **expertise**— even those with very senior jobs, or in positions of fame or great responsibility—are often willing to speak with high school students.

"They want to teach," Fettner says. "They want to **mentor**."

Cruz says students can find **mentors** by asking counselors for help or simply by picking up the phone and asking an adult for an informational interview.

"We place students in 'experientials' to spend time with **professionals** doing what they think they want to do," Cruz says about her career program. "That's a maker or breaker because they say, 'I can't wait to get there' or 'Are you out of your mind? I don't want to do that.'

"I had one student I was going to put . . . in a pathology lab at a hospital. He had been watching [the TV show] *CSI.* I explained to him what he would be seeing and doing on a daily basis, and he said, 'That's dead people. I don't want to be around dead people.' So we got him a different experience.

On the Rise

These are expected to be the fastest-growing jobs in the United States between 2006 and 2016, according to the U.S. Bureau of Labor Statistics.

Job	Education Required	Median Wages (2006)	Projected Growth
Audio/video equipment technicians	On-the-job training	$34,840	12,000 jobs
Truck drivers	On-the-job training, certification	$37,270	193,000
Personal and home health-care aides	On-the-job training	$20,460	384,000
Surgical technologists	Post-secondary certificate	$36,080	21,000
Court reporters	Post-secondary certificate	$45,610	5,000
Environmental engineering technicians	Associate degree	$40,560	5,000
Occupational therapist's assistants	Associate degree	$42,060	6,000
Registered nurses	Associate degree	$57,280	587,000
Accountants/auditors	Bachelor's degree	$54,630	226,000
Computer software engineers (applications)	Bachelor's degree	$79,780	226,000
Computer systems analysts	Bachelor's degree	$69,760	146,000
Database administrators	Bachelor's degree	$64,670	34,000
Elementary school teachers	Bachelor's degree	$45,570	209,000
Multimedia artists and animators	Bachelor's degree	$51,350	23,000
Network systems and data communications analysts	Bachelor's degree	$64,600	140,000
Physician assistants	Master's degree	$74,980	18,000
Lawyers	Professional degree	$102,470	84,000

"He may be doing physical therapy with disabled children; that's what he wants. . . . So being able to see what's going on in that area is a real valuable thing, if you can get it."

What skills that employers are looking for might surprise readers?

"I've interviewed 5,000 people, asking them, 'When you're hiring, what are the skills you're most looking for?'" Kivland says. "One of the top ones that keeps coming out is **resilience**. They're looking for people with a story of bouncing back from setbacks."

Prospective employers are often interested in hearing about instances in which you were put in uncomfortable or unfamiliar situations and found ways to **adapt**. Kivland calls such instances situations that "have stretched you in a way." Kivland strongly recommends that high school students take a few risks and try activities that might seem a little uncomfortable. For example, a less assertive student might seek a leadership role in an organization, or a student gifted in math or science might sign up for a drama or writing class to get an experience that he or she hasn't mastered yet.

"Place yourself in situations where you can lead and follow. Place yourself in situations where you take a risk," says Kivland. "You might not win, but it will give you an opportunity of **resiliency**, of bouncing back."

Registered nurse is one of the fastest-growing jobs in the United States.

Learning That Works

by Joe Klein

1 Clyde McBride is one of those everyday saints who, without much fanfare, go about the work of changing, and sometimes saving, the lives of children. He teaches agricultural science on the Navajo reservation in Kayenta, Arizona. He's a memorable-looking fellow, with his cowboy hat, horsehide tie, and a body like a giant sack of flour perched on tiny toothpick legs. His most notable characteristic, though, is his **persistence**. When a new school superintendent arrived in town a few years ago, McBride parked himself on the guy's doorstep. "He came in and gave me the 'I have a dream' speech," says superintendent Harry Martin. "I told him I'd think about it, but he wouldn't let me think about it. He was bugging me three, four times a week about it."

McBride's dream was a state-of-the-art agricultural-sciences building with two veterinary operating theaters—one for small animals

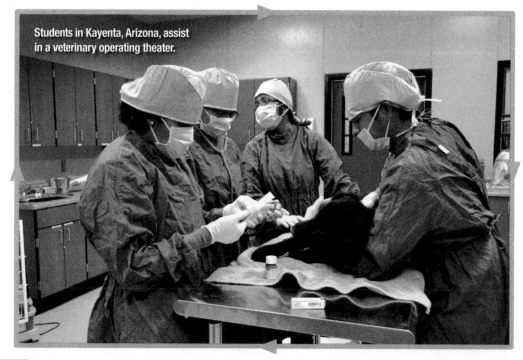

Students in Kayenta, Arizona, assist in a veterinary operating theater.

and one for large ones—to train Navajo kids to be veterinary aides and **technicians** and perhaps even to start a few of them down the road to becoming veterinarians. "I thought it was a waste of money and time," Martin told me. "I'm an old English teacher. I was very skeptical about vocational education. We needed to be drilling them on basic skills. But McBride said he'd make a believer out of me. And he did."

> ## "It's an alternative way to teach them math, science, and reading. They love it."

Two years later, with the $2.4 million agricultural- and **technical**-sciences building up and running, Martin says, "It's without doubt the best program we have. It's an alternative way to teach them math, science, and reading. They love it. They're attentive, working hard, hands on." McBride imports veterinarians from around the country to visit the reservation and work with the 226 students, who

assist in both operating theaters, prepping animals for surgery and learning how to suture, draw blood, and give injections. The veterinary clinic has become a valued resource on the reservation, but more than that, the academic results have been spectacular. "Nearly every one of these kids passed the state comprehensive test we give to 17-year-olds in Arizona," Martin told me. "Less than about 40 percent of my non-vocational-education students passed."

❷ Vocational education used to be where you sent the dumb kids or the supposed misfits who weren't suited for classroom learning. It began to fall out of fashion about 40 years ago, in part because it became a civil rights issue: voc-ed was seen as a form of segregation, a convenient dumping ground for minority kids in Northern cities. "That was a real problem," former New York City schools chancellor Joel Klein told me. "And the voc-ed programs were pretty awful. They weren't training the kids for specific jobs or for certified skills. It really was a waste of time and money."

Unfortunately, the education **establishment's** response to the voc-ed problem only made things worse. Over time, it morphed into the theology that every child should go to college (a four-year liberal-arts college at that) and therefore every child should be required to pursue a college-prep course in high school. The results have been awful. High school dropout rates continue to be a national embarrassment. And most high school graduates are not **prepared** for the world of work. The unemployment rate for recent high school graduates who are not in school is a stratospheric 33 percent. The results for even those who go on to higher education are brutal: four-year colleges graduate only about 40 percent of the students who start them, and two-year community colleges graduate less than that, about 23 percent. "College for everyone has become a matter of political correctness," says Diane Ravitch, a professor of education at New York University. "But according to the Bureau of Labor Statistics, less than a quarter of new job openings will require a bachelor of arts degree. We're not training our students

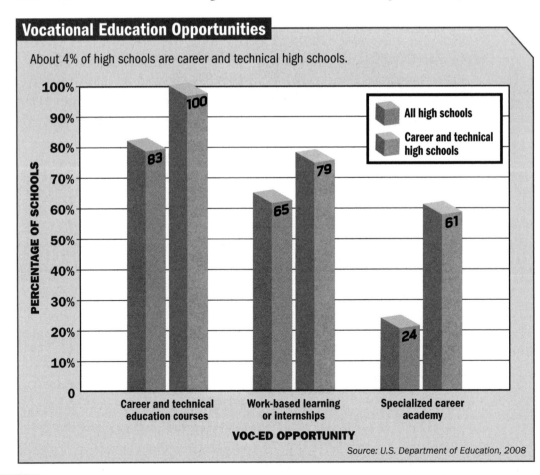

Vocational Education Opportunities

About 4% of high schools are career and technical high schools.

Legend:
- All high schools
- Career and technical high schools

Career and technical education courses: 83, 100
Work-based learning or internships: 65, 79
Specialized career academy: 24, 61

PERCENTAGE OF SCHOOLS

VOC-ED OPPORTUNITY

Source: U.S. Department of Education, 2008

for the jobs that actually exist." Meanwhile, the United States has begun to run out of welders, glaziers, and auto mechanics—the people who actually keep the place running.

> **About 27 percent of the students in Arizona opt for the tech-ed path, and they are more likely to score higher on the state's aptitude tests, graduate from high school, and go on to higher education.**

In Arizona and more than a few other states, that is beginning to change. Indeed, the old **notion** of vocational education has been stood on its head. It's now called career and **technical** education (CTE), and it has become a pathway that even some college-bound advanced-placement students are pursuing. About 27 percent of the students in

Arizona opt for the tech-ed path, and they are more likely to score higher on the state's aptitude tests, graduate from high school, and go on to higher education than those who don't. "It's not rocket science," says Sally Downey, superintendent of the spectacular East Valley Institute of Technology in Mesa, Arizona, 98.5 percent of whose students graduate from high school. "It's just finding something they like and teaching it to them with rigor." Actually, it's a bit more than that: it's developing training programs that lead to jobs or recognized certification, often in partnership with local businesses. Auto shop at East Valley, for example, looks a lot different from the old jalopy that kids in my high school used to work on. There are 40 late-model cars and the latest in diagnostic equipment, donated by Phoenix auto dealers, who are desperate for trained **technicians**. "If you can master the computer-science and electronic components," Downey says, "you can make over $100,000 a year as an auto mechanic."

Arizona has another, rather unusual advantage. Its state education superintendent, John Huppenthal, went to high school in Tucson on the voc-ed track. "It was considered the path for losers, but I didn't know any better," says Huppenthal, a Republican who was elected to the statewide post. "I came from a family of machinists. I didn't know anybody who'd gone to college, and I was happy in wood shop. I remember making a chess set, a very complicated project that really made mathematics come alive for me." He also happened to be a state-champion wrestler with pretty good test scores, and his coach encouraged him to study engineering at Northern Arizona University. "I really believe that some form of CTE is essential for a world-class education," he says. "Most students respond better to a three-dimensional learning process. It's easier to learn engineering by actually building a house—which my family did when I was a kid, by the way—than sitting in a classroom figuring out the process in the abstract. Some students can respond to two-dimensional learning, but most respond better when it's hands on. Every surgeon needs to know how to sew, saw, and drill."

❸ Precise statistics are sparse; it's difficult to keep track of students after they leave high school. But Carolyn Warner, a former Arizona schools chancellor, says tech-track students "are more **focused**, so they're more likely to graduate from two- and four-year colleges. Those who graduate from high school with a certificate of **technical expertise** in a **field** like auto repair or welding are certainly more likely to find jobs."

Still, Huppenthal finds vocational school is a tough sell to the state's education **establishment**. "It doesn't have the prestige of a college-prep course," he says, "and it costs a lot more than two-dimensional education to do it right." Traditionally, Democrats have tended to be opposed on ideological grounds. They're the strongest believers in college for everyone. Republicans are **reluctant** to spend the money on state-of-the-art equipment like the veterinary center on the Navajo reservation, although some concede that CTE programs that **prepare** students for actual jobs are a good idea. "It's like walking in a hurricane," says Huppenthal. "You know where you want to be going, but the winds keep pushing you off course."

But CTE is beginning to produce its own weather systems—human tornadoes like McBride and Downey, the superintendent at East Valley, who is smart and passionate and extremely pushy, constantly working the business community in Phoenix for help in starting training programs. There are 38 programs on her campus, with more coming. There are firefighter, police, and EMT programs; a state-of-the-art kitchen for culinary-services training; and welding (which can pay $48 per hour), aeronautics, radio-station, marketing, and massage-therapy instruction. ("We have a lot of resorts around here," Downey explains, "and our students often work part time as masseurs to earn money for college.") Almost all of these courses lead to **professional** certificates in addition to high school diplomas, and many of the students are trained by employers for needed **technical specialties**. None of her 3,200 students are full time. They spend half a day, usually afternoons, at East Valley and receive academic training at 35 different home high schools in the mornings.

"Look at this," Downey says as she shows me a fully stocked medical laboratory. "We got $1.5 million from Veterans Affairs to run a program for surgical assistants, and they gave us a teacher to teach it." The premedical and -nursing students here are dressed in scrubs. Downey barges into a classroom and begins polling the students. "How many of you are going on to some form of higher education?" Almost everyone's hand goes up. "How many of you are taking advanced-placement programs in your home high schools?" A scattering of hands. "How many of you have had to make sacrifices to come here?" Again, a forest of hands. Most of the sacrifices involve

East Valley Institute of Technology students use the latest technology to diagnose engine problems.

hours of travel and having to give up extracurricular activities. "And how many of you were discouraged from doing this by your local high schools?" About half. The home high schools tend to have the standard **biases** against vocational education—that it's a waste of time, that it takes away from the academic experience.

"The public school system also has a civic purpose," says Jonathan Zimmerman, an education historian at New York University, citing a common academic argument against vocational education. "You're not just **preparing** people to work. You're **preparing** people to be citizens. In a democracy, you need citizens who can think critically." But people with jobs, especially skilled jobs, tend to be better citizens than those without them. And the teamwork involved in the training programs at East Valley and on the Navajo reservation tends to help create a sense of community. "In my home high school, you're sitting in a room with 30 other students who don't care, trying to pay attention to a teacher who doesn't care," says Aaron Pietryga, who is training to become a firefighter. "But [East Valley] is like my family. Most of the kids at my home school don't have any idea

what I'm doing in the afternoon, and when I explain it to them, they say, 'Wow, you're doing all that cool stuff, and you're going to college. Why didn't I know about that?'"

On a recent chilly morning at the Navajo reservation, McBride was giving Huppenthal and me a hands-on tour of his veterinary facility. Husband-and-wife veterinarians from Pittsburgh had volunteered their services for a few days and were spaying a dog in the small-animal operating theater, with the help of students in blue surgical

In 2009, 18 percent of high school graduates earned at least one credit in consumer and culinary services.

scrubs. "They're very good," says Sharon Wirtz, one of the vets. "They have an exceptional feel for this, especially with the larger animals," like sheep and horses. Students were suturing bananas and injecting oranges with red dye for practice. Recently a pack of wild dogs attacked some sheep on the reservation, and McBride took some students to care for them. "Some of these kids suture better than I do," he says. "It brings tears to my eyes."

But his real triumph wasn't in teaching the Navajo the **technical** skills. These students also knew how to make an impression; they had learned the soft skills necessary to be good employees. They looked you in the eye, introduced themselves and shook your hand (which was universally true at East Valley as well). This was striking, given the history of depression and despair on the reservation. "These kids are thirsty. All you've got to do," McBride says, eyes brimming, "is let them drink."

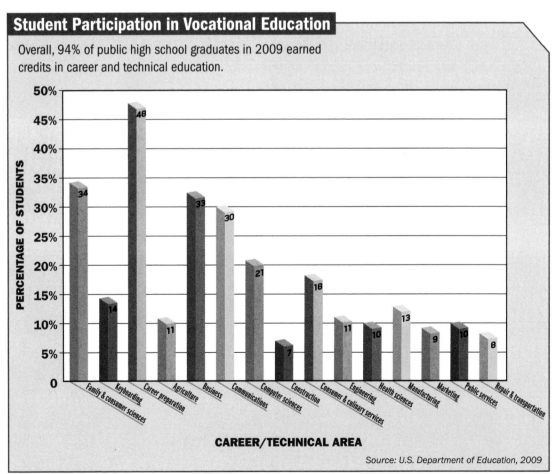

Student Participation in Vocational Education

Overall, 94% of public high school graduates in 2009 earned credits in career and technical education.

Source: U.S. Department of Education, 2009

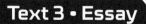

Text 3 • Essay

Educating the Next Steve Jobs

How can schools teach students to be more innovative?
Offer hands-on classes and don't penalize failure.

by Tony Wagner

Most of our high schools and colleges are not **preparing** students to become **innovators**. To succeed in the 21st-century economy, students must learn to analyze and solve problems, collaborate, persevere, take calculated risks, and learn from failure. To find out how to encourage these skills, I interviewed scores of **innovators** and their parents, teachers, and employers.

What I learned is that young Americans learn how to **innovate** most often despite their schooling—not because of it.

Though few young people will become brilliant **innovators** like Steve Jobs, most can be taught the skills needed to become more **innovative** in whatever they do. A handful of high schools, colleges,

Innovative schools use hands-on projects to teach problem solving.

and graduate schools are teaching young people these skills—places like High Tech High in San Diego, the New Tech high schools (a network of 86 schools in 16 states), Olin College in Massachusetts, the Institute of Design (d.school) at Stanford, and the MIT Media Lab. The culture of learning in these programs is radically at odds with the culture of schooling in most classrooms.

> *Young Americans learn how to innovate most often despite their schooling—not because of it.*

In most high-school and college classes, failure is penalized. But without trial and error, there is no **innovation**. Amanda Alonzo, a 32-year-old teacher at Lynbrook High School in San Jose, California, who has **mentored** two Intel Science Prize finalists and 10 semifinalists in the last two years—more than any other public school science teacher in the United States—told me, "One of the most important things I have to teach my students is that when you fail, you are learning." Students gain lasting self-confidence not by being protected from failure but by learning that they can survive it.

The university system today demands and rewards **specialization**. Professors earn tenure based on research in narrow academic **fields**, and students are required to declare a major in a subject area. Though **expertise** is important, Google's director of talent, Judy Gilbert, told me that the most important thing educators can do to **prepare** students for work in companies like hers is to teach them that problems can never be understood or solved in the context of a single academic discipline. At Stanford's d.school and MIT's Media Lab, all courses are interdisciplinary and based on the exploration of a problem or new opportunity. At Olin College, half the students create interdisciplinary majors like "Design for Sustainable Development" or "Mathematical Biology."

Learning in most conventional education settings is a **passive** experience: the students listen. But at the most **innovative** schools, classes are "hands-on," and students are creators, not mere consumers. They

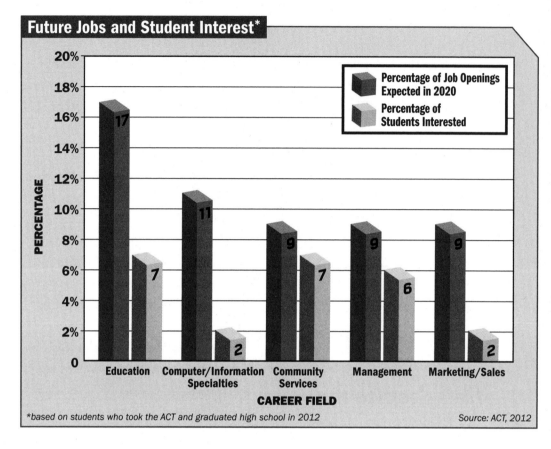

Future Jobs and Student Interest*

Legend:
- Percentage of Job Openings Expected in 2020
- Percentage of Students Interested

Y-axis: **PERCENTAGE** (0 to 20%)

X-axis: **CAREER FIELD**

Career Field	Job Openings Expected in 2020	Students Interested
Education	17	7
Computer/Information Specialties	11	2
Community Services	9	7
Management	9	6
Marketing/Sales	9	2

*based on students who took the ACT and graduated high school in 2012

Source: ACT, 2012

acquire skills and knowledge while solving a problem, creating a product, or generating a new understanding. At High Tech High, ninth graders must develop a new business concept—imagining a new product or service, writing a business and marketing plan, and developing a budget. The teams present their plans to a panel of business leaders who assess their work. At Olin College, seniors take part in a yearlong project in which students work in teams on a real engineering problem supplied by one of the

college's corporate partners.

In conventional schools, students learn so that they can get good grades. My most important research finding is that young **innovators** are intrinsically motivated. The culture of learning in programs that excel at educating for **innovation** emphasize what I call the three P's—play, passion, and purpose. The play is discovery-based learning that leads young people to find and pursue a passion, which evolves, over time, into a deeper sense of purpose.

Mandating that schools teach **innovation** as if it were just another course or funding more charter schools won't solve the problem. The solution requires a new way of evaluating student performance and investing in education. Students should have digital portfolios that demonstrate progressive mastery of the skills needed to **innovate**. Teachers need **professional** development to learn how to create hands-on, project-based, interdisciplinary courses. Larger school districts and states should **establish** new charter-like laboratory schools of choice that pioneer these new approaches.

Creating new lab schools around the country and training more teachers to **innovate** will take time. Meanwhile, what the parents of future **innovators** do matters enormously. My interviews with parents of today's **innovators** revealed some fascinating patterns. They valued having their children pursue a genuine passion above their getting straight As, and they talked about the importance of "giving back." As their children matured, they also encouraged them to take risks and learn from mistakes. There is much that all of us stand to learn from them.

Innovation programs should emphasize "play, passion, and purpose."

SHOULD EVERYONE HAVE TO TURN OUT TO VOTE?

Data File

The most important thing you get on your 18th birthday isn't a cake or presents—it's the right to vote! Will you exercise it?

Vote: It's Your Right

Currently, every American **citizen** age 18 and over has the right to vote—but that wasn't always the case. In the 200+ years since the US Constitution was written, three Amendments were added to grant and protect the rights of certain groups to vote.

- Amendment XV, ratified February 3, 1870, states that the right to vote cannot be denied on account of "race, color, or previous condition of servitude."

- Amendment XIX, ratified August 18, 1920, grants all women over age 21 the right to vote.

- Amendment XXVI, ratified July 1, 1971, sets the minimum voting age for all **citizens** to 18 years of age.

(Source: National Archives, www.archives.gov)

By the Numbers

- In the 2008 Presidential election, 231,229,580 American **citizens** were eligible to vote, but only 56.8%, or 132,618,580 voters, turned up at the polls.

- Young people ages 18–29 make up 21% of the voting population. In 2008, 51.1% of young people voted, accounting for 17.1% of the total vote.

(Source: Associated Press Election Research Group, George Mason University, 2012)

Telling Americans to Vote, or Else

by William A. Galston

Jury **duty** is mandatory; why not voting? The idea seems vaguely un–American. Maybe so, but it's neither unusual nor **undemocratic**. And it would ease the intense partisan polarization that weakens our capacity for self-government and public trust in our governing **institutions**.

Thirty-one countries have some form of mandatory voting, according to the *International Institute for Democracy and Electoral Assistance*. The list includes nine members of the Organization for Economic Cooperation and Development and two-thirds of the Latin American nations. More than half back up the legal requirement with an enforcement mechanism, while the rest are content to rely on the moral force of the law.

Despite the prevalence of mandatory voting in so many **democracies**, it's easy to dismiss the practice as a form of statism that couldn't work in America's individualistic and libertarian political culture. But consider Australia, whose

Many Americans can't afford to wait in long lines at the polls.

VOTE HERE
★ ★ ★ ★

political culture is closer to that of the United States than that of any other English-speaking country. Alarmed by a decline in voter turnout to less than 60 percent in 1922, Australia adopted mandatory voting in 1924, backed by small fines (roughly the size of traffic tickets) for nonvoting, rising with repeated acts of nonparticipation. The law established permissible reasons for not voting, like illness and foreign travel, and allows **citizens** who faced fines for not voting to defend themselves.

The results were remarkable. In the 1925 election, the first held under the new law, turnout soared to 91 percent. In recent elections, it has hovered around 95 percent. The law also changed **civic** norms. Australians are more likely than before to see voting as an **obligation**. The negative side effects many feared did not materialize. For example, the percentage of ballots intentionally spoiled or completed randomly as acts of resistance remained on the order of 2 to 3 percent.

Proponents offer three reasons in favor of mandatory voting. The first is straightforwardly **civic**. A **democracy** can't be strong if its **citizenship** is weak. And right now American **citizenship** is attenuated—strong on rights, weak on responsibilities. There is less and less that being a

citizen requires of us, especially after the abolition of the draft. Requiring people to vote in national elections once every two years would reinforce the principle of reciprocity at the heart of **citizenship**.

> **Mandating voting nationwide would go counter to our traditions (and perhaps our Constitution) and would encounter strong state opposition.**

The second argument for mandatory voting is **democratic**. Ideally, a **democracy** will take into account the interests and views of all **citizens**. But if some regularly vote while others don't, officials are likely to give greater weight to participants. This might not matter much if nonparticipants were evenly distributed through the population. But political scientists have long known that they aren't. People with lower levels of income and education are less likely to vote, as are young adults and recent first-generation immigrants.

Changes in our political system have magnified these disparities. During the 1950s and '60s, when turnout rates were much higher, political parties reached out to **citizens** year-round. At the local level these parties, which reformers often criticized as "machines," connected even **citizens** of modest means and limited education with neighborhood **institutions** and gave them a sense of participation in national politics as well. In its heyday, organized labor reinforced these effects. But in the absence of these more organic forms of political mobilization, the second-best option is a top-down mechanism of universal mobilization.

Mandatory voting would tend to even out disparities stemming from income, education and age, enhancing our system's inclusiveness. It is true, as some object, that an enforcement mechanism would impose greater burdens on those with fewer resources. But this makes it all the more likely that these **citizens** would respond by going to the polls, and they would stand to gain far more than the cost of a traffic ticket.

The third argument for mandatory voting goes to the heart of our current ills. Our low turnout rate pushes American politics toward increased polarization. The reason is that hard-core partisans are more likely to dominate lower-turnout elections, while those who are less fervent

In the United States, all citizens age 18 and older have the right to vote, but voting is not mandatory.

about specific issues and less attached to political organizations tend not to participate at levels proportional to their share of the electorate.

> **Mandatory voting would tend to even out disparities stemming from income, education and age, enhancing our system's inclusiveness.**

A distinctive feature of our **constitutional** system—elections that are quadrennial for president but biennial for the House of Representatives—magnifies these effects. It's bad enough that only three-fifths of the electorate turns out to determine the next president, but much worse that only two-fifths of our **citizens** vote in House elections two years later. If events combine to energize one part of the political spectrum and dishearten the other, a relatively small portion of the electorate can shift the system out of all proportion to its numbers.

Some observers are comfortable with this asymmetry. But if you think that today's intensely polarized politics impedes governance and exacerbates mistrust—and that is what most Americans firmly (and in my view rightly) believe—then you should be willing to consider reforms that would strengthen the forces of conciliation.

Imagine our politics with laws and **civic** norms that yield near-universal voting. Campaigns could devote far less money to costly, labor-intensive get-out-the-vote efforts. Media gurus wouldn't have the same **incentive** to drive down turnout with negative advertising. Candidates would know that they must do more than mobilize their bases with red-meat rhetoric on hot-button issues. Such a system would improve not only electoral politics but also the legislative process. Rather than focusing on symbolic gestures whose major purpose is to agitate partisans, Congress might actually roll up its sleeves and tackle the serious, complex issues it ignores.

The United States is not Australia, of course, and there's no guarantee that the similarity of our political cultures would produce equivalent political results. For example, reforms of general elections would leave untouched the distortions generated by party primaries in which small numbers of voters can shape the choices for the entire electorate. And the United States Constitution gives the states enormous power over voting procedures. Mandating voting nationwide would go counter to our traditions (and perhaps our Constitution) and would encounter strong state opposition. Instead, a half-dozen states from parts of the country with different **civic** traditions should experiment with the practice, and observers—journalists,

social scientists, **citizens'** groups and elected officials—would monitor the consequences.

We don't know what the outcome would be. But one thing is clear: if we do nothing and allow a politics of passion to define the bounds of the electorate, as it has for much of the last four decades, the prospect for a less polarized, more effective political system that enjoys the trust and confidence of the people is not bright.

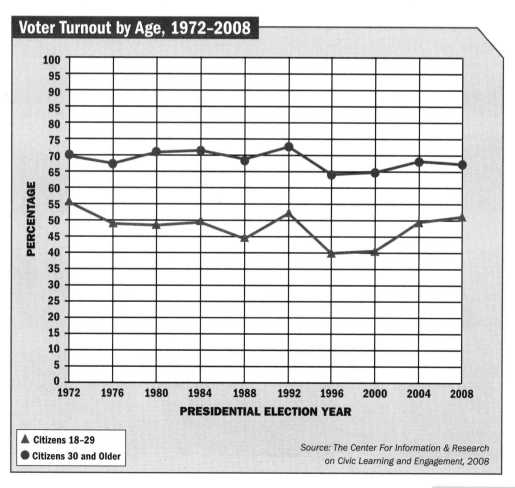

Voter Turnout by Age, 1972–2008

▲ Citizens 18–29
● Citizens 30 and Older

Source: The Center For Information & Research on Civic Learning and Engagement, 2008

What Does It Mean to Be an American Citizen?

by Lee H. Hamilton

We are here today because the success of any **democracy** is determined by the participation of its **citizens**.

Lincoln asked whether a nation devoted to the values of liberty, equality, justice and opportunity "so conceived . . . can long endure." In these words, he told us a truth about our **democracy**—that its survival is never guaranteed, and that its success demands wisdom, action and even vigilance from American **citizens**. Thus, I focus my remarks today on the basic question: what does it mean to be an American **citizen**?

The success of a democracy is determined by the participation of its citizens.

❶ What Do We Owe?

First, what do we as American **citizens** owe? We begin with gratitude. As many have said, the joy of being an American is the joy of freedom and opportunity. We have been bequeathed freedom, justice and opportunity from the deeds and commitments—even the spilled blood—of Americans who came before us. We did not earn the inheritance.

> People are voting less; paying less attention to their civic responsibility; . . . participating less and complaining more.

This nation of unequaled wealth and power, of freedom and opportunity, was given to us. But no matter how rich and powerful it becomes, America is not and never will be a finished project. It is always aborning.

You and I are handed a work in progress, one that can evolve for good or for ill. American **democracy** makes a wager on its **citizens**. The deal is simple—with freedom comes **obligation**, with liberty comes **duty**. If that deal is not kept, **democracy** is threatened. Lincoln said at Gettysburg: "It is for us the living, rather, to be dedicated here to the unfinished work which they who fought here have thus far so nobly advanced." He spoke of a new birth of freedom so that government of, by, and for the people would not perish.

You and I must learn and we must teach our young the words we live by: the Constitution, the Declaration of Independence, and the other grand documents of American history. And we must learn and teach about the **institutions** that bring life and permanence to these words and deeds so familiar to us, so that they may fulfill Lincoln's charge.

Democracy is not fixed like a monarchy. It is **dynamic**. **Democracy** reflects the will and above all the action of each generation of American **citizens**. So what do we owe? As Americans we owe a profound debt of gratitude for the actions of those who **preceded** us, and we owe those who will follow an America that is even greater and more beautiful than it was transmitted to us.

❷ Why Are We Concerned?

But I am concerned, as I know you are. Why are we concerned?

We are concerned because too many Americans lack a basic understanding of our **democracy**, our **institutions**, our **representative democracy**, our **obligation** to those who came before, and what each of us can and must do to preserve the blessings of liberty.

> Civic engagement is your way of influencing for the better your neighborhood, community, state and nation.

A multitude of surveys confirm our concerns. But we don't even need to look at surveys or statistics to know that political participation and **civic** engagement is down basically across the board. People are voting less; paying less attention to their **civic** responsibility; ignoring the great lessons of the American experiment; participating less and complaining more.

There is a sense, particularly among many young people, that being an American **citizen** is no big deal, with no **obligation** attached to it, an endeavor not particularly worthy of their time and talent. I know of young people in Indiana who when asked about the meaning of Memorial Day respond by saying that it is the day that pools are opened, or the occasion for the Indianapolis 500 auto race.

All of us are aware of a disconnect between people and their elected **representatives**. People do not trust them. People think they do the bidding of powerful interests. People think they are not **relevant** to their day-to-day lives. People think that **citizenship** is hollow.

You and I are concerned because we know that if we are apathetic, passive, and cynical about our **democracy**, then we will invite leaders who abuse power. There is an old observation: a society of sheep must in time beget a government of wolves.

You and I are concerned because we stand on a precipice. If American **citizens** increasingly become

Which is the Most Powerful Place in America?

☐ THE WHITE HOUSE

☐ THE PENTAGON

☐ THE U.S. CAPITOL

THE VOTING BOOTH

VOTE

A political cartoon draws attention to a political issue, often in a humorous way.

disengaged, then the entire American **democratic** enterprise is at risk. Indeed, sometimes I wonder about whether our **democracy** can continue as we know it if **civic** participation continues to decline as it has.

Why Engage?

Why should you and I and others engage in **civic** activity?

We have plenty of important things to worry about doing our jobs, paying our bills, taking care of our families. No doubt, these private interests are **civic** virtues in their own right.

We are good in this country at speaking out for and protecting our individual interests. But all of us can benefit from giving at least some of our attention to advancing the public interest, or as the founding fathers called it the common good.

Look around you. Many things need to be done in your

community and country. Perhaps you are upset by the actions of your **representative**. Or the school that your children attend. Or the quality of your health care. Or the conditions of the roads that you drive on. Or even our nation's foreign policy.

> # I know people who vote, walk out of the booth, and say and believe that their civic duty has been fully discharged.

Don't misunderstand me. Tending your own business and the affairs of your family is important. But **civic** engagement is your way of influencing for the better your neighborhood, community, state and nation. If you and I become involved, our cynicism will dissipate and our morale improve. We may even see life become better, richer, and fuller for our fellow **citizens**.

I know people who vote, walk out of the booth, and say and believe

that their **civic duty** has been fully discharged. Voting is important but not enough. Do you know who does not disengage when the voting is done? Interest groups. They begin their work the day after an election; they know that's when the real work begins. They know it and so should the rest of us.

If you are upset about the influence exerted by special interests, if you are upset about the actions of a public official, if you are upset about the condition of your local school, even if you are upset about a pothole in front of your house, **civic** engagement is a way of taking action to make your corner of the world better. What do we have on our agenda that is more important?

The key to good governance is simple: it is to hold power accountable. **Civic** engagement does just that. We engage because it improves our **democracy**, and it is the only way to make our government **responsive** to the people.

❸ What Can We Do?

How, then, do we engage?

If you ask them, most Americans want to be better people living in better communities, a better state, and a better nation. Often, they want to become involved but don't know how, don't know where to go, whom to talk to, what to do.

Thus the job of **civic** education is not complete if we teach only its importance; we must be shown how to engage, how to participate, how to get off the sidelines and into the action.

This may seem overwhelming at first. But I like the attitude of the builder who said: I cannot solve the world's problems, but I can help build this house.

A constituent of mine was a diabetic. He approached me one day many years ago because he had no idea what was in the food on sale at the grocery store, and his health depended upon it.

But he did more than just talk to me. He spoke around the community to whomever would listen; visited and wrote letters to all kinds of officials, county commissioners, state legislators, other members of Congress. Thanks to him, and many people of like mind and action,

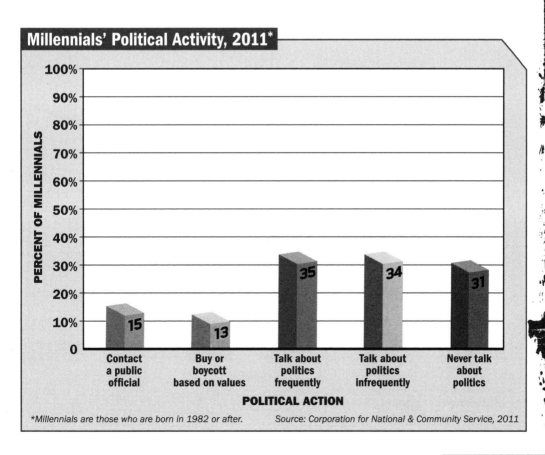

Millennials' Political Activity, 2011*

*Millennials are those who are born in 1982 or after.   Source: Corporation for National & Community Service, 2011

consumers now have meaningful labels on the food that they buy.

We would all like to engage to **resolve** the big problem. Fixing health care. Saving social security. Changing the tax code. Defending our nation against its enemies. Some of us have those opportunities, but most of us don't.

All of us can engage most effectively through small, incremental changes. A school is rebuilt. Ramps for the handicapped are carved into street corners. A safety signal goes up in a dangerous intersection. A worthy, young disadvantaged student enters medical school. A young woman steps into the world with more opportunity than her mother.

These are not insignificant examples. They save and improve lives and communities. The actions of my constituent and countless American **citizens** like him made many American lives healthier. This is the wellspring of our American

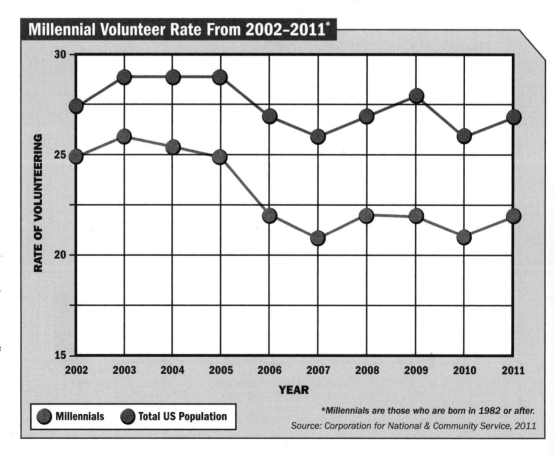

Millennial Volunteer Rate From 2002–2011*

*Millennials are those who are born in 1982 or after.
Source: Corporation for National & Community Service, 2011

democracy: countless small actions that make a better nation.

We engage by looking around us, seeing something that needs fixing, and doing something about it:

- We can stay more informed about issues in our own communities, as well as the issues of the state and nation.

- We can run for elective office or work for candidates of our choice.

- We can vote in elections and hold each of our **representatives** accountable—from the president on down to a town council or commissioner.

- We can join **institutions** of service—be it the Peace Corps, the armed services, Americorps, or local uniformed services.

- We can volunteer for charitable causes and organizations.

- We can join the sometimes messy, rough and tumble dialogue of **democracy** by writing letters to local papers or elected officials, asking questions or advocating positions.

- We can give speeches or ask questions about why things cannot be better across the street or across the world.

- We can organize petition drives or letter writing campaigns.

- We can join—or begin— organizations that reflect our views and enlarge our collective voice.

I cherish the citizen who says: I belong here; I have a role to play; I have a contribution to make.

If you know your community— the problems that need addressing; the different kinds of people (not just the people like you); the issues; who is in charge; who has the power to get a message out; who can assemble people together—I can assure you, you will engage. Set goals; craft messages; organize; and when successful share the credit.

Civic engagement is the greatest antidote for cynicism; it is also a great—maybe the best—lesson of **democracy**.

When we become engaged in community life—we no longer feel distant from the centers of power and decision-making. We come to understand our own communities, and appreciate how we can influence change. Perhaps most important, we gain an appreciation for the hard work of **democracy**: how to understand different points of view and forge a **consensus** behind a course of action toward a solution in a complex, busy and diverse society.

If we engage, we lessen the distance between ourselves and those who govern. And we gain understanding and appreciation for our country that can only make it and the ongoing experiment of American **democracy** stronger.

Conclusion

You and I believe that **democracy** is the most worthy form of government. And we know that **democracy** cannot thrive—indeed, cannot exist—without the active participation of **citizens**.

So we must get into our bones the ideas of **representative democracy**: the consent of the governed, the

Attending a school board meeting is one way to get involved in your community.

institutions of **democracy** in our nation, the necessity of participation, and the avenues for action that are open to all of us.

Our engagement brings out the very best within us. Our nation demands not only our competence, but also our passion.

President Kennedy's words resonate through the years: "In your hands, my fellow **citizens**, more than mine, will rest the final success or failure of our course. Ask not what your country can do for you, ask what you can do for your country."

I cherish the **citizen** who says: I belong here; I have a role to play; I have a **contribution** to make.

What does it mean to be an American **citizen**? It means that we are blessed to be part of this nation; we are concerned about a shortage of **civic** awareness and engagement; and we should act to effect meaningful change and accountable government through countless avenues for **civic** action. Above all, it means we are responsible for tending to our own **democracy**, making it work for all and transmitting it to our children better than we inherited it.

You accept the responsibility of an American **citizen**. Fortunately there are many more Americans like you but not enough. Our charge is to spread this message anew to all Americans.

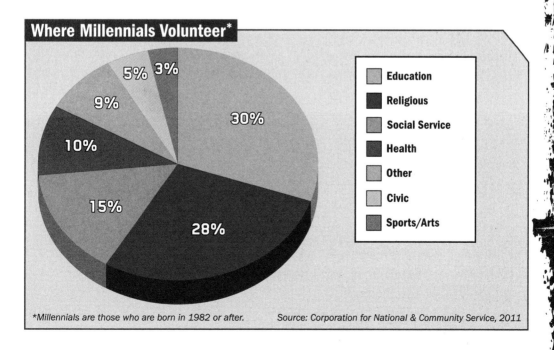

Where Millennials Volunteer*

- Education
- Religious
- Social Service
- Health
- Other
- Civic
- Sports/Arts

30%
28%
15%
10%
9%
5%
3%

*Millennials are those who are born in 1982 or after.

Source: Corporation for National & Community Service, 2011

The Light That Shined from Ruleville (from the novel *Countdown*)

by Deborah Wiles

Fannie Lou Townsend Hamer was child number twenty.

She had fourteen older brothers and five older sisters, so she was the baby, born on a farm in the Hill Country of Mississippi in 1917, the same year as JFK, more than fifty years after the end of the Civil War.

So Fannie Lou, a black child, was born into freedom. Or was she?

Her parents were sharecroppers on the farm. The whole family took care of one another and worked from daybreak to dusk to bring in the cotton harvest for the plantation owner. When Fannie was a baby, one of her brothers accidentally dropped her and the fall broke her leg. There was no money for a doctor, so the bone wasn't set properly, and Fannie Lou walked with a limp for the rest of her days.

Fannie Lou Townsend Hamer dedicated her life to securing voting rights for African Americans.

When she was two years old, her family moved to Sunflower County, to another plantation, this one in the rich soil of the Mississippi Delta, where Fanny Lou grew up and lived for the rest of her life. Ruleville was the name of the town.

The Delta land was as flat as a door as far as the eye could see. Every now and then, a tree grew in the middle of a field, like a scarecrow with eight or ten limbs, like arms, akimbo. "Hangin' trees," the sharecropper families called them.

Like other sharecropper families living and working on plantations, Fannie Lou's family was paid to bring in the cotton, but they weren't paid much, and they weren't paid fairly. They did all the work, but stayed poor, poor, poor. And in the Delta, there were no other jobs.

Most Negroes knew they were being cheated, but they rarely said anything when it came time for pay-day—it was too dangerous. White people owned the Delta, owned Mississippi, and owned the American South. They made the rules, and they depended on their cheap labor— the black sharecroppers—to make them their fortunes.

(There were poor white families, too.)

It had been that way ever since the days of slavery and most white people in Mississippi wanted it to stay that way. They didn't want the Negroes to have any power.

(What were they afraid of?)

So they made RULES.
Some were written into law.
Some were unspoken.

And the Negroes, who wanted to keep themselves and their families safe, learned to obey these rules.

Negroes were second-class **citizens**. They couldn't go to the same good schools as white children, couldn't eat in the same restaurants, couldn't swim in the town pools or shop in the same stores or use the same bathrooms. They could cook and clean and sew and take care of white folks. And that's what many of them did, those who didn't work on the plantations in the fields.

Most of them were not **registered** to vote.

They knew that asking for change was dangerous. Pushing for fairness had found many a black man hanging by his neck from a hangin' tree, out in the middle of the Delta, or scraping the bottom of a riverbed nearby.

So there was no money for shoes. In the summer Fannie Lou went barefoot. In the winter, her mother tied rags around Fanny Lou's feet to keep them warm, but Fannie got so cold, she would stand in the places where the cows had been resting, in order to warm her feet.

Many black folks in Mississippi couldn't read or write or do their sums because they spent so much time in the cotton fields they didn't go to school. Even when they could go to school, they didn't have the proper books or clothes or shoes.

Fannie loved school. She was a spelling whiz and a fine reader. She loved to read so much, she would hop off the cotton wagon if she saw a scrap of newspaper by the side of the dirt road, and sometimes she'd go through the trash at the plantation owner's house, looking for words in print to read.

And she sang—my, that Fannie could sing! She loved church songs, she loved the songs of the cotton fields, and she loved to sing for her family at night after everyone got home and sat on the front steps shelling peas or roasting peanuts. Her favorite song was "This Little Light of Mine."

THIS LITTLE LIGHT OF MINE, I'M GONNA LET IT SHINE!

She started working in the cotton fields when she was six years old. By the time she was thirteen, she could pick two hundred pounds of cotton in a week. She grew up, married Pap Hamer, and started sharecropping with him in the Delta. And she grew sick and tired of being treated like a second-class **citizen**. So sick and tired that, when the Negroes from the cities north and south began **organizing** for change, she wanted to hear what they had to say.

So, in 1961, the same year that Alan Shepard became the first

Fannie Lou Hamer speaks to supporters of the Mississippi Freedom Democratic Party in Washington, DC.

American in space, the same year that John F. Kennedy was sworn in as the thirty-fifth president of the United States, the same year that the anti-Castro forces invaded Cuba at the Bay of Pigs, and the same year that the movie *King of Kings* was released . . .

Fannie attended a meeting at a church in Ruleville where she heard the speakers—black **organizers** she had never met (Bob Moses, Jim Farmer, James Bevel)—say that she, Fannie Lou Hamer, had a right to vote in this country and to make a change in America.

*"I didn't know that a Negro could **register** and vote!"*

Who will go with us on the bus,
to the courthouse, to **register** to vote?

Fannie Lou's hand was the first in the air.

"Had it up as high as I could get it."

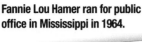
Fannie Lou Hamer ran for public office in Mississippi in 1964.

CANDIDATES TO RUN ON JUNE 2---

Mrs. Victoria Gray   James M. Houston   Mrs Fannie Lou Hamer   Rev. John Cameron

THE STUDENT VOICE

VOL. 5 NO. 13   STUDENT VOICE, INC.   6 Raymond Street, N. W.   Atlanta, Georgia 30314   JUNE 2, 1964

NEGROES RUN IN MISS.

FOUR RUN ON FREEDOM SLATE

JACKSON, MISS. - Mississippi's voters - over 95% of them white - may not elect any of the four Negro candidates running in the June 2 primary but each is determined to go to Washington to represent the state in Jan. 1965.

The four - Mrs. Victoria Gray, and the Rev. John Earle Cameron, both of Hattiesburg; Mrs. Fannie Lou Hamer of Ruleville, and James M. Houston of Vicksburg - asked the state's voters to make a choice they've never been asked to make before 'to choose between the white, segregationist regular Democrats and four civil-rights conscious Negroes running under the banner of the Freedom Democratic Party.

None of the Negro candidates expects to win Tuesday's election, but all hope to be seated in the House and Senate in Jan. 1965.

Although Negroes are more than 40% of the state's population, only some 20,000 Negroes are registered voters. Registered whites make up 95% of the electorate. CONTINUED ON PAGE 4

"I guess if I'd had any sense, I'd have been a little scared—but what was the point of being scared? The only thing they could do was kill me, and it seemed they'd been trying to do that a little bit at a time since I could remember."

Fannie Lou Hamer became a community **organizer**. The plantation owner kicked her off the farm, and Pap followed her as soon as the harvest was in.

"Find the Lady who sings the hymns," said Bob Moses. The civil rights movement became her home.

After three tries, Fannie successfully **registered** to vote. Then she rode on the buses and helped others **register**. She worked as a field secretary for the Student Nonviolent Coordinating Committee—SNCC—and the Congress for Racial Equality—CORE—the **organizations** that sent the **organizers**.

She was arrested,

she was beaten,

she was ridiculed,

she was shot at.

She was GALVANIZED.

She spoke with fire from her heart in a voice that rolled like thunder. She sang to her compatriots, to calm them. She led them in the songs of the movement—the civil rights movement. *Ain't Gonna Let Nobody Turn Me 'Round!*

Fannie Lou became fearless.

HIDE IT UNDER A BUSHEL—NO!
I'M GONNA LET IT SHINE!

"We're tired of all this beatin', we are tired of takin' this. It's been a hundred years and we're still being beaten and shot at, crosses are still being burned, because we want to vote. But I'm goin' to stay in Mississippi and if they shoot me down, I'll be buried here."

She worked with the Freedom Riders who came to Mississippi for Freedom Summer in 1964—most of them young white students from college campuses in the North. She helped train them, just as she had been trained.

Soon, everyone knew who she was, even President Kennedy and, after he died, President Johnson. Fannie Lou was indeed **registered** to vote, and she wanted all black people to have the right to **register** and vote. To vote was to have the power to change things. She traveled to the Democratic National Convention in Atlantic City, New Jersey, in 1964, and in front of television cameras, so all of America could see her and hear her, she said,

"All my life I've been sick and tired. Now I'm sick and tired of being sick and tired."

and

"I question America. Is this America? The land of the free and the home of the brave?"

Fannie Lou Hamer changed her destiny when she raised her hand as high as she could get it that night in Ruleville and said YES. She changed the destiny of thousands upon thousands of people, black and white, and every color under the sun. She demanded human rights for all. And because she did, she helped change the world.

"In 1962 nobody knew that I existed. Then one day, the thirty-first of August, I walked off the plantation. From that time up until now I met a lot of people. I met a lot of great people, both blacks and whites. People that we have walked together, we have talked together, we've cried together."

Even of the people who beat her, she said, "Baby, you have to love 'em."

"I feel sorry for anybody who would let hate wrap them up. Ain't no such thing as I can hate anybody and hope to see God's face."

In 1964, President Lyndon Johnson signed the Civil Rights Act of 1964, which assured every American, EVERY American, the right to every public place—every public drinking fountain, restroom, restaurant, school, and more.

In 1965, President Johnson signed into effect the Voting Rights Act. Martin Luther King, Jr. was in attendance.

In 1965, President Johnson signed into effect the Voting Rights Act, which gave every American **citizen** of age the right to **register** and vote. He appeared on television and said,

> *"I speak tonight for the dignity of man and the destiny of **democracy**. . . . The Constitution says that no person shall be kept from voting because of his race or his color. We have all sworn an oath before God to support and to defend that Constitution. We must now act in obedience to that oath. . . . Wednesday I will send to Congress a law designed to **eliminate** illegal **barriers** to the right to vote. . . ."*

Fannie Lou had said it all along:

> *"Live up to the creed, live up to the Declaration of Independence, the Bill of Rights."*

In 1977, Fannie Lou Townsend Hamer died of cancer, and probably of complications from the beatings she had received fourteen years earlier as she struggled for her civil and human rights. She was fifty-nine years old.

> *"Nobody's free 'til everybody's free."*

And the struggle continues.

Meet the Author

DEBORAH WILES

Born: May 7, 1953, in Mobile, Alabama

Background: Deborah's father was an air force pilot, and her family was stationed in Washington, DC, during the 1960s. She has vivid memories of ducking and covering under her school desk during air raid drills at the time of the Cuban Missile Crisis. She also sang in the Glee Club, was a champion speller, and hated Field Day.

On how *Countdown* became a "documentary novel": "Storytelling encompasses so much more than words on paper. And when I was researching this story, there was a rich mother lode of material—photographs, cartoons, songs, newspaper clippings. All these things were another way of telling the story."

IS FAILURE THE SECRET OF SUCCESS?

Data File

What can we learn from failure? Is it better to get it right the first time or to struggle along the way?

Famous Failures

Many people have failed along the way to great success:

- George Washington almost lost his job as commander of the Continental Army before becoming the first president of the United States.

- Steve Jobs was fired from Apple, the company he helped start, before returning to oversee the creation of the iPod, iPhone, and iPad.

- Three record labels dropped Katy Perry, who went on to sell more than 48 million songs.

- Albert Einstein was expelled from school before going on to win the Nobel Prize in Physics.

- No colleges offered Jeremy Lin a basketball scholarship and no NBA teams drafted him. Then he had a breakout season and signed a $25 million contract in 2012.

(Source: Scholastic Scope, 2012)

Learning to Be Helpless

Studies have shown that animals and humans can develop "learned helplessness." This is when someone accepts a painful or annoying situation instead of trying to change it. In an experiment published in 1975:

- People were divided into three groups.

- Group one heard a loud noise they could stop by pushing a button. Group two heard the noise and could not stop it. Group three didn't hear anything.

- The next day, all three groups heard a noise they could turn off. People from groups one and three quickly figured out how to stop it. In group two, about two-thirds of people didn't try to stop the noise.

Dr. Martin E.P. Seligman's research shows that the difference in the one-third of people who don't learn to be helpless is that they are more optimistic. They see failures as "temporary, local, and changeable."

(Source: Harvard Business Review, 2011)

Talent Isn't Fixed and Other Mindsets That Lead to Greatness

by Jocelyn K. Glei

In the creative world, we spend a lot of time talking about "talent." It's that special sauce—a certain style, a certain perspective, a certain aesthetic. If you've got it, you've got it. And if you don't, well . . . it can't really be taught, right?

Not exactly.

According to Stanford University's Carol Dweck, the psychologist behind the much-praised book *Mindset: The New Psychology for Success*, the attitude that we bring to our creative work—and to mentoring our juniors—can play a huge role in shaping just how much of our inborn talents we realize.

If we believe that someone's talent is fixed—including our own—we are effectively writing off any options for growth. But if we believe that talent, or intelligence, or any other ability, **evolves** as a result of how much effort we put in, the opportunities are endless.

I chatted with Dweck to learn more about how a "growth mindset" can impact creative **achievement** on a personal and a professional level.

When we're children, we think we can do anything. Especially in terms of creativity, we don't think about our skill set as being limited. Why does that stop at a certain age?

It can actually stop as soon as we become conscious of ourselves. We start thinking that our mistakes are failures—and that these failures tell us and other people that we are not competent, that we are not worthy. This process can happen quite young.

Fast-forwarding into adulthood and being out in the working world, how does being afraid of failure impact people's ability to be creative?

It makes you afraid of being judged. Now, what innovation or creativity requires is that you do things that haven't been done before. And that you stick to them until you succeed. If you have a "fixed mindset," which is this idea that you have a certain amount of limited ability, you are afraid to choose hard tasks. You think: "What if I don't succeed? People will think I'm not as smart as I want to be, as I want them to think I am."

When we give adults the choice to go back to something they've already done well, or something they haven't done as well at, the ones with the

Psychologist Carol Dweck says that a "growth mindset" can help people be more innovative and creative.

fixed mindset go back to things they already know. In that scenario, you are not stretching forward, or stepping out of your comfort zones. You are really just concerned with looking smart all the time.

Adults in a fixed mindset also think that great effort, great struggle, means that you are not smart. It's the notion that: "If I were smart, if I were talented, it would just come to me." But people in a "growth mindset" enjoy the effort, welcome the struggle. They understand that innovation requires it.

How do these two mindsets play out when we're dealing with setbacks? When we don't succeed right away?

In a growth mindset, you don't always welcome the setback, you were hoping to move forward, but you understand that it's information on how to move forward better next time. It is a **challenge** that you are **determined** to surmount. In a fixed mindset, a setback calls your ability into question.

Everything is about: "Am I smart? Am I not smart?" But if you're always managing your image to look smart, you're not taking on the hardest tasks, you're not thinking about them in the most innovative ways, and you're not sticking to things that don't work right away.

How can we bring a "growth mindset" to giving people feedback on creative projects?

Whether we are praising or **criticizing**, my work suggests that you focus on the process, not on the person. So if there is a success, even a great success, you don't say, "You're a genius! You really have talent!" because it puts people into a fixed mindset.

And then it makes them afraid of doing hard things or of making mistakes, which will dampen future creativity or innovation. If you are giving negative feedback, it should be about the process rather than the person. So you can praise what was good about the process, but then you can also analyze what was wrong about the process and what the person can do in order to increase the likelihood of succeeding next time.

> **"People in a 'growth mindset' enjoy the effort, welcome the struggle."**

Could you give me an example of how that language would actually play out if I were giving someone feedback?

A fixed mindset approach would be saying something like: "This project turned out amazing. You're a genius. I knew you had the talent. This is proof of it." As opposed to a growth mindset approach of "Wow, this project turned out fantastically well. I loved the way you mobilized the team, the way you kept everyone focused, the way you brought it to fruition, the way you made everybody feel the ownership." These are things you can replicate and that you should replicate the next time. Whereas, when I say, "You're a genius!" . . . how do you reproduce that over and over?

And what about when you need to give someone criticism? Or point out an area that needs work?

As I mentioned, when you are giving **criticism**, you need to carefully **critique** the process someone engaged in and discuss what skills they need to learn and improve.

But I've also fallen in love with a new word—"yet." You can say to someone who fell short: "You don't seem to have this," but then add the word "yet." As in, "You don't seem to have these skills…yet." By doing that, we give people a time perspective. It creates the idea of learning over time. It puts the other person on that learning curve and says, "Well, maybe you're not at the finish line but you're on that learning curve and let's go further." It's such a growth mindset word.

In the creative world, the notion of talent (as opposed to effort) is emphasized constantly. How can we break out of that cycle?

First, there is some great research on changing managers' mindsets by Peter Heslin. In one workshop, managers were asked to think of examples from their own lives that illustrated a growth mindset—like "What are some things you thought you could never do, and then you did them?" Or writing a letter to someone who had been doing well but was now hitting a period of struggle, and mentoring that person in terms of a growth mindset.

> **"Start seeing all these things—challenges, setbacks, role models—as learning opportunities."**

The researchers then followed these managers for at least six weeks and compared them to managers who did not have the growth mindset training. The first thing they noticed was that the managers who had the growth mindset training were now much more open to feedback from their employees. They were also less likely to make snap judgments about who has talent and who doesn't.

They also found that the managers became much more willing to mentor. Because if you're in a fixed mindset and you believe that some people have it and some people don't, you think, well, "I will just wait and see who has it and who doesn't. Cream rises to the top." But if you have a growth mindset, you understand that "Hey, I'm in the business of growing talent, helping it develop, not just sitting back and judging it."

And how can an individual start to change his or her own mindset?

One thing I tell people is, just as a first step, start listening to the fixed mindset voice in your head. It's always there, telling you: "Oh, are you sure you want to do this? You might make mistakes and, you know, people will find you out. You're not going to look like the genius you want to look like." Or if you start struggling, the fixed mindset says, "Oh, I told you so, but it's not too late, you can still get out and save face." For a while just do that, just start listening to the fixed mindset voice keeping score. And then over time: start talking back.

If you're with someone who is tremendously able and successful, think: "What can I learn from this person? Yes, maybe I feel a little intimidated but this person could be a great mentor. I could learn a lot. Maybe I could get to know them, maybe they could take me under their wing. Maybe I want to know more about getting from where I am to where they are. What are their secrets?"

Start talking back and seeing all these things—**challenges**, setbacks, role models—as learning opportunities. Do it most of all if you still feel threatened, because we all have a little part of ourselves that is a little shy, a little threatened. Do it anyway! And see how well it works.

This interview is from www.99u.com, a website that aims to provide insights on making ideas happen.

Fixed vs. Growth Mindset

Fixed Mindset		Growth Mindset
"Some people are born smarter than others."	INTELLIGENCE	"Intelligence and talents can develop over time."
"I'm just going to stick to what I already do well."	CREATIVITY	"I'm going to try something new, and I'll learn something whether it succeeds or fails."
"I'll never be good at this."	MISTAKES	"Making a mistake means I can improve next time."
"If it's difficult, I'm not smart. I should give up."	EFFORT	"Struggling means that I'm learning and it's something worth doing."
"You're so smart!"	PRAISE	"Your hard work made the project successful."

Angela Duckworth and the Research on "Grit"

by Emily Hanford

1 Before she was a psychology professor, Angela Duckworth taught math in middle school and high school. She spent a lot of time thinking about something that might seem obvious: the students who tried hardest did the best, and the students who didn't try very hard didn't do very well. Duckworth wanted to know: What is the role of effort in a person's success?

Now Duckworth is an assistant professor at the University of Pennsylvania, and her research focuses on a personality **trait** she calls "**grit**." She defines **grit** as "sticking with things over the very long term until you master them." In a paper, she writes that "the **gritty** individual approaches **achievement** as a marathon; his or her advantage is stamina."

Duckworth's research suggests that when it comes to high **achievement**, **grit** may be as essential as intelligence. That's a significant finding because for a long time, intelligence was considered the key to success.

Intelligence "is probably the best-measured **trait** that there is in all of human psychology," says Duckworth. "We know how to measure intelligence in a matter of minutes."

But intelligence leaves a lot unexplained. There are smart people who aren't high **achievers**, and there are people who **achieve** a lot without having the highest test scores. In one study, Duckworth found that smarter students actually had less **grit** than their peers who scored lower on an

Psychology professor Angela Duckworth developed a Grit Scale that helps explain why some students do better than others.

intelligence test. This finding suggests that, among the study participants—all students at an Ivy League school— people who are not as bright as their peers "**compensate** by working harder and with more **determination**." And their effort pays off: the **grittiest** students—not the smartest ones—had the highest GPAs.

The Grit Test

Duckworth's work is part of a growing area of psychology research focused on what are loosely called "noncognitive skills." The goal is to identify and measure the various skills and **traits** other than intelligence that contribute to human development and success.

Duckworth has developed a test called the "Grit Scale." You rate yourself on a series of 8 to 12 items. Two examples: "I have overcome setbacks to conquer an important **challenge**" and "Setbacks don't discourage me." It's entirely self-reported, so you could game the test, and yet what Duckworth has found is that a person's **grit** score is highly **predictive** of **achievement** under **challenging** circumstances.

At the elite United States Military Academy, West Point, a cadet's **grit** score was the best **predictor** of success in the rigorous summer training program known as "Beast Barracks." **Grit** mattered more than intelligence, leadership ability, or physical fitness.

> **When it comes to high achievement, grit may be as essential as intelligence.**

At the Scripps National Spelling Bee, the **grittiest** contestants were the most likely to advance to the finals—at least in part because they studied longer, not because they were smarter or were better spellers.

❷ Grit and College Completion

Angela Duckworth is now turning her attention to the question of **grit** and college completion. In a study funded by the Gates Foundation, Duckworth and a number of other researchers are trying to understand what **predicts** college persistence among graduates of several high-performing urban charter school networks: YES Prep Public Schools in Houston, Mastery Charter

Schools in Philadelphia, Aspire Public Schools in California, and Achievement First Schools in Connecticut.

These charter school networks serve mostly students from low-income and minority families. The schools were founded to close the "**achievement gap**" between these students and their higher-income peers. The **ultimate** goal of these charter school networks is to get students to go to college and earn degrees.

The charter schools have succeeded in providing strong academic preparation. Most of their students go to college. Yet the students graduate from college at lower rates than would be expected based on their academic preparation.

The charter schools want to know why that is. Angela Duckworth wants to know if **grit** has anything to do with it.

Duckworth's previous research shows that people who have "some college" but no degree are lower in **grit** than people who have college degrees. Does that mean the charter school students who are not making it

So far, 40 percent of YES Prep graduates have earned bachelor's degrees within six years of high school graduation.

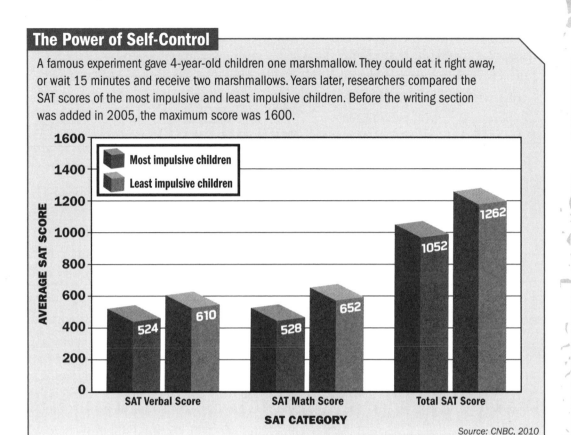

The Power of Self-Control

A famous experiment gave 4-year-old children one marshmallow. They could eat it right away, or wait 15 minutes and receive two marshmallows. Years later, researchers compared the SAT scores of the most impulsive and least impulsive children. Before the writing section was added in 2005, the maximum score was 1600.

Legend:
- Most impulsive children
- Least impulsive children

AVERAGE SAT SCORE

SAT Verbal Score: 524, 610
SAT Math Score: 528, 652
Total SAT Score: 1052, 1262

SAT CATEGORY

Source: CNBC, 2010

through college are lacking **grit**? And if that's the case, can **grit** be learned?

These are complicated questions, and the answers aren't in yet. Duckworth says there are a number of things to think about before jumping to the conclusion that students who don't finish college *aren't* **gritty**. Many factors contribute to college success, including money, what colleges students go to, and what Duckworth calls "social-psychological" barriers. She says low-income and minority students often feel out of place on college campuses, especially more elite colleges where the majority of students are upper-income, white, and have college-educated parents. Duckworth thinks a sense of social belonging may be key to persisting through college. One of her research goals is to "sharpen insights" about the psychological barriers that prevent well-prepared students from completing degrees—and to test **interventions** that might help students overcome those barriers.

But Duckworth thinks **grit** is likely a significant factor when it comes to college completion among the charter school students she is studying. That's because **grit** is a particularly helpful **trait** when it comes to **challenging** experiences, and for the charter school students, college tends to be a **challenging** experience.

> # Grit is a particularly helpful trait when it comes to challenging experiences, and for the charter school students, college tends to be a challenging experience.

Most of the students are first generation; their parents didn't go to college—in many cases, no one in their family has any experience with higher education. College can be a difficult and confusing experience even for people who come from college-educated families, but for first-generation students, college is like learning a new language, says Tenesha Villanueva, a codirector of alumni programs at YES Prep Public Schools in Houston.

"It's like going to a foreign country and trying to navigate systems and programs that you have never come in contact with before," says Villanueva.

When first-generation students come up against **obstacles** in college, they have no one in their families to turn to for help, says Villanueva. College-educated families provide their students with support that many students and families may not even be aware of, but it's a powerful force that helps propel students through college. Villanueva says first-generation students are at a disadvantage.

Not only do first-generation students lack the kind of family support that can help them overcome **obstacles** in college, they also tend to face more **obstacles** than higher-income students from college-educated families, according to Villanueva and her colleagues at YES Prep. They may have trouble with money or financial aid paperwork. A lot of the students have to work while going to school. Many live at home and have family obligations, such as taking care of siblings or grandparents and helping to pay the bills. Research shows all of these things make going to college harder and increase the chances a student will quit.

YES Prep graduated its first class of seniors 11 years ago. So far 40 percent of the students have earned bachelor's degrees within six years of finishing high school. Twenty-eight percent have dropped out. The rest are still in college, **gritting** it out years after they were expected to finish.

❸ The Grittiest College Students

When college is hard, **grit** helps, according to Angela Duckworth's research.

In fact, people who succeed in getting associate's degrees are, on average, more **gritty** than people

Sample Character Strengths Profile

Grit and other character traits can change over time. The VIA Survey measures 24 character strengths. Here is a sample report.

Strength	
Honesty	
Creativity	
Perspective	
Judgment	
Prudence	
Love of Learning	
Bravery	
Curiosity	
Leadership	
Appreciation of Beauty and Excellence	
Fairness	
Humility	
Hope	
Perseverance	
Social Intelligence	
Teamwork	
Forgiveness	
Self-regulation	
Humor	
Love	
Gratitude	
Kindness	
Zest	
Spirituality	

SIGNATURE
MIDDLE
LESSER

who get bachelor's degrees, according to Duckworth's research. It takes as much **grit** to get an associate's degree as it does to get a Ph.D.

"Graduating from a two-year college versus a four-year college is a much greater difference than people might imagine," says Duckworth.

Community colleges are full of students who are a lot like the students at YES Prep and the other urban charter schools Duckworth is studying: first-generation college students from poor families who have to balance work and family while going to school. The community college dropout rate is high.

"If you're going to get through a two-year college where the attrition rate is 50 or maybe even 75 percent, maybe you do need more **grit** to surmount all those **obstacles**," says Duckworth.

Learning to Be Gritty

It's not clear what makes some people **grittier** than others, but Angela Duckworth believes **grit** is something people can probably learn.

She says every human quality that has been studied has proven to be

"You can see a child be exceptionally self-disciplined about their basketball practicing, and yet when you see them in math class, they give up at the slightest frustration," says Duckworth.

affected at least in part by a person's **environment**—even intelligence. In addition, people change over time.

"Think about things about your personality, like 'I'm a pretty extroverted person,'" says Duckworth. "Well, how fixed is that?"

> ## It takes as much grit to get an associate's degree as it does to get a Ph.D.

It turns out a personality **trait** like extroversion can change a lot over a person's life. "If you look at large population data, people get more or less extroverted over time," says Duckworth. "There's no reason to think that **grit** is any different."

She believes **grit** can wax and wane in response to experiences. In addition, people might be **gritty** about some things and not others.

"You can see a child be exceptionally self-disciplined about their basketball practicing, and yet when you see them in math class, they give up at the slightest frustration," says Duckworth.

Donald Kamentz, director of college initiatives at YES Prep, says students he's worked with are some of the **grittiest** people he's ever met. They "deal with things and **persevere** through situations that most people would find insurmountable," he says.

He's known students who get jobs to pay the bills when their parents are laid off, or figure out how to get the electricity back on when the power company shuts it off.

"And then they go to college and they're struggling with financial aid or their financial aid didn't come through and they don't know what to do," he says. Some of them drop out when **confronted** with these kinds of **challenges**. He says they're not **gritty** enough when it comes to college.

A question for YES Prep and other charter schools in Duckworth's study is not necessarily how to get students to be **gritty**, but how to get them to be **gritty** about college completion.

"Which experiences do we give kids to get them in the direction of more **grit** and not less?" asks Duckworth.

One of the goals of Duckworth's research is to figure this out. Her current project began in the fall of 2011 and is scheduled to wrap up in 2014.

The Brave Boys of Greensboro
Would you risk your life to sit down for lunch?

by Spencer Kayden

Characters

Narrators 1, 2, and 3
(N1, N2, N3)

Martin Luther King Jr.

The Greensboro Four, 17-year-old college freshmen:

  Ezell Blair Jr.

  Joe McNeil

  David Richmond

  Franklin McCain

Cashier

Waitress

Mr. Harris, manager of
  Woolworth's

Counter maid

Customer

Police officer

Jo Spivey, female news reporter

Bettye, black college student

*Names in **bold** are major roles.*

PROLOGUE

N1: Slavery officially ended in 1865, but nearly 100 years later, prejudice against African Americans continued. Many states in the South had Jim Crow laws, unfair rules that required black Americans to go to separate schools, live in separate neighborhoods, and eat in separate restaurants from white Americans.

N2: In the 1950s, a movement was started to change that system. Blacks and whites worked together—organizing **demonstrations**, marches, and other peaceful protests. But they risked their lives to do so. They were arrested and attacked. Some had their homes burned down. Others were even murdered.

N3: One of the great leaders of this civil rights movement was Dr. Martin Luther King Jr., who said . . .

MARTIN LUTHER KING JR.: **Nonviolence** is a powerful and just weapon, which cuts without wounding and ennobles the man who wields it. It is a sword that heals.

N1: This is the story of four teenagers who took up that sword.

From left, Joe McNeil, Franklin McCain, and two friends sit at the lunch counter on day two of the sit-in.

SCENE 1

N2: It is February 1, 1960, a Monday afternoon in Greensboro, North Carolina.

N3: Four African American teenagers meet up at their college library.

EZELL: So, are we really going to do this?

JOE: Absolutely. I'm wearing my best suit.

DAVID: I didn't sleep at all last night.

EZELL: Neither did I.

FRANKLIN: We can't back out now.

JOE: Does everyone know the plan?

DAVID: We go in and buy something, like regular customers.

EZELL: This is never going to work.

JOE: What's the worst thing that could happen?

DAVID: We get arrested.

FRANKLIN: Or we end up with our heads split open, brought back to campus in pine boxes.

JOE: Let's stick to the plan, and remember, whatever happens, no violence.

N1: The four boys walk downtown, their gazes fixed straight ahead. They round the corner onto Elm Street and walk into Woolworth's Department Store.

N2: They have been to this store many times before, but this time their hearts are pounding.

N3: David approaches the stationery counter.

DAVID: I'd like to buy these pencils, please.

CASHIER: That will be 50¢.

N1: David pays and takes his receipt.

N2: Franklin and Joe nod at each other and silently walk to the lunch counter.

N3: They sit down. David and Ezell join them.

N1: The waitress stares at them with shock and amazement.

N2: The room gets deadly quiet, except for the squeak of the swivel stool as Ezell sits on his hands to stop them from shaking.

SCENE 2

N3: Flashback to 14 hours earlier. The boys are in their college dormitory.

Dr. Martin Luther King Jr. believed in nonviolence and led protests demanding civil rights.

DAVID: So, Joe, how was your trip?

JOE: I went to New York to see my family. Coming back South, I was okay until I got to the bus station in Greensboro. I tried to buy a sandwich, but they wouldn't serve me.

FRANKLIN: I am getting tired of being treated like a second-class citizen.

DAVID: I heard they might close the public pool rather than allow black people to swim there.

JOE: How have our parents lived like this for so long?

FRANKLIN: You know, we stay up every night talking about how we don't like the way blacks are treated. Maybe we're hypocrites.

DAVID: What do you mean?

FRANKLIN: We're all talk, talk, talk, and no action. Maybe it's time to do something.

EZELL: How can the four of us change the entire city of Greensboro?

FRANKLIN: We have to get people's attention and show them how unjust **segregation** is.

DAVID: Well, we can't boycott a store because they'll throw us in jail and say we're taking business away.

JOE: What if we go somewhere that's for whites only, and try to give them our business?

EZELL: Like where?

JOE: A place where the racism is obvious, like Woolworth's Department Store. We can shop there, but we aren't allowed to sit down at the lunch counter.

EZELL: You're suggesting we sit where no black person has ever sat before and ask to be served?

JOE: Exactly.

EZELL: They'll beat us up!

FRANKLIN: Not if we are quiet and respectful. We will dress nicely and we won't do anything to provoke them.

DAVID: Let's do it tomorrow, before I lose my nerve.

EZELL: They'll never serve us.

FRANKLIN: Then we will sit at the counter until they do.

SCENE 3

N1: At the lunch counter that next afternoon, the four boys sit, waiting to see if they will be arrested or worse.

N2: For many minutes, nothing happens. The waitress ignores them. White patrons glare, but no one moves.

FRANKLIN: Excuse me, ma'am. We'd like to be served.

WAITRESS: I'm sorry. I can't serve you here.

JOE: We would just like a cup of coffee, please.

WAITRESS: You can go to the stand-up counter downstairs.

N3: She walks away. A black counter maid comes over.

COUNTER MAID: What are you boys doing? You're stirring up trouble. Making it harder for the rest of us. Go back to campus. Please!

N1: She storms off. The manager comes over.

MR. HARRIS: Is there a problem?

EZELL: No, sir. We'd like to order some coffee, please.

MR. HARRIS: Boys, I can only serve you downstairs.

DAVID: You served me when I bought pencils a few minutes ago, just five feet from here.

MR. HARRIS: As I said, you can order whatever you want downstairs.

DAVID: Thank you, but we prefer to sit here with your other customers.

MR. HARRIS: You can't sit here.

FRANKLIN: Is it against the law?

MR. HARRIS: No. It's just the way things are.

FRANKLIN: Do you think "the way things are" is just?

MR. HARRIS: Doesn't matter what I think. It's store **policy**.

JOE: With respect, sir, we don't agree with your **policy**. And we're going to sit here until we're served.

N2: An elderly white customer finishes her doughnut and walks toward them.

N3: Franklin steels himself for her harsh words.

N1: The woman puts her hands on Franklin's shoulders.

CUSTOMER: Boys, I am so proud of you. I just wish you had done this 10 years ago.

N2: The boys swell with pride and sit a little taller knowing someone is on their side.

N3: By now a crowd has gathered, staring and pointing.

N1: A police officer walks in.

EZELL (whispering)**:** We're done for.

N2: The officer stalks up and down the aisle behind them, menacingly slapping his nightstick into his palm.

DAVID (whispering)**:** He could crack our skulls with that.

N3: The officer talks to Mr. Harris.

POLICE OFFICER: What's the situation?

MR. HARRIS: Everybody knows that the lunch counter is for whites only.

POLICE OFFICER: I can't arrest them for just sitting there. Have they started any fights or said anything inflammatory?

MR. HARRIS: No, they have been nothing but polite.

POLICE OFFICER: Then I suggest you close the store early. This will all blow over in a day or two.

MR. HARRIS: I wouldn't be too sure about that.

SCENE 4

N1: The next morning, the boys arrive at Woolworth's with two more friends.

N2: They sit at the lunch counter for most of the day. No one serves them.

N3: Meanwhile, word quickly spreads about what the boys are doing. Newspaper reporters and TV crews show up.

JO SPIVEY: Boys, what brought this on?

From left, David Richmond, Franklin McCain, Ezell Blair Jr., and Joe McNeil leave Woolworth's.

"Freedom Riders" protested discrimination on interstate buses. They were nonviolent but encountered mobs who sometimes burned buses.

DAVID: I was taught that we live in a democracy, that all men are created equal. But we are not treated as equals. Far from it.

JOE: Have you ever wondered why we can only sit in the balcony at the movie theater? Why we have to sit at the back of the bus or go to separate schools?

N1: Some white hecklers threaten the boys, who ignore them and continue sitting.

JO SPIVEY: Do you think you are accomplishing anything with this sit-in?

EZELL: It is time for someone to wake up and change the situation, and we decided to start here.

SCENE 5

N2: On day three, several dozen students from the boys' school and other colleges come to Woolworth's.

BETTYE: We're here to sit with you in solidarity.

FRANKLIN: We need all the help we can get. But you will probably be abused and called nasty names.

BETTYE: We can handle it.

N3: The students take out their books, sit at the counter, and start studying.

JO SPIVEY: Are you compromising your schoolwork to be here?

FRANKLIN: We promised each other a few things: not to miss classes, to behave courteously, and if punched or taunted, we turn the other cheek.

JO SPIVEY: Has there been any progress?

JOE: Woolworth's headquarters in New York issued a statement saying that their **policy** is to abide by local custom.

JO SPIVEY: So it's up to Mr. Harris?

EZELL: It seems so. He's just waiting for us to get tired and go away. But we have no intention of doing that.

SCENE 6

N1: On day four, 300 students show up at Woolworth's.

JO SPIVEY: Seems like people are starting to listen.

FRANKLIN: I've got a pal in Raleigh. He read about us in the paper and says they are planning a sit-in, too.

JO SPIVEY: You boys sure are getting a lot of attention.

DAVID: Yeah, but not all of it's good. Last night I got a phone call at the dorm . . . some guy said if I came back to Woolworth's, I was a dead man.

JOE: But we are not going to be stopped by threats.

N2: By the end of the week, more than 1,000 students, black and white, converge on Woolworth's.

N3: By the end of the month, sit-ins are taking place in more than 30 communities in seven states.

N1: And by July, the lunch counter at Woolworth's is officially **desegregated**.

N2: Soon, every restaurant in Greensboro is serving all customers, regardless of race.

EPILOGUE

N3: Today, more than 50 years later, those four teenage boys are known as the "Greensboro Four." They are remembered as heroes of the civil rights movement.

EZELL: Lots of people never stop to wonder why things are the way they are, no matter how bad. They just accept it.

FRANKLIN: It was our moral obligation to take a stand.

JOE: My grandchildren find it hard to believe that there was a time when a black person couldn't walk into a restaurant and order a cup of coffee.

DAVID: There's no better feeling in the world than standing up for what you believe is right and true.

ACADEMIC LANGUAGE HANDBOOK

Use the academic language frames in this handbook as a reference during academic discussions.

The **heading** states the overall type of discussion or interaction.

Look for the **"If" statement** that most closely describes the specific type of interaction.

Look for examples of completed frames in **speech bubbles**.

ACADEMIC LANGUAGE HANDBOOK

SYN / LANGUAGE

Facilitating Discussion
Collaborate to have a discussion in a small group.

If you want to ask a group member to add an idea . . .
- So _____, what's your (experience/suggestion)?
- So _____, what's your (perspective/point of view)?
- _____, what (reason/example) did you come up with?

If you want to ask a group member about a word . . .
- So _____, are you familiar with the word _____?

If you want to share word knowledge with the group . . .
- No. I have never heard the word _____.
- I'm unfamiliar with the word _____.
- I recognize _____. It has something to do with _____.
- I can use _____ in a sentence. For example, _____.
- I know the word _____. It means _____.

If you want to share word knowledge with the class . . .
- My group members are unfamiliar with the word _____.
- We recognize the word _____, but we would benefit from a review of the meaning.
- We recognize the word _____, but we would benefit from a review of how to use it in a sentence.
- We think _____ means _____.

> No. I have never heard the word "deficit."

Language Tip
Follow "has something to do with . . ." with a noun or verb phrase that you associate with the word.
For example, "I recognize metabolism. It has something to do with your body."

Stating Perspectives
Give your opinion about an issue or a topic.

If you want to share your opinion . . .
- In my (opinion/experience), _____.
- From my (perspective/point of view) _____.
- I know from experience that _____.
- Based on my experience, _____.

> From my perspective, I believe that schools should start later to accommodate teens.

Introducing Evidence
Provide supporting evidence for your claim.

If you want to give text evidence . . .
- For (example/instance), _____.
- To illustrate, _____.
- As an illustration, _____.
- In the text, _____.
- The (text/author) _____.
- In addition, the text _____.
- The data (show/prove) _____.
- (Studies/Recent findings) (show/prove) _____.

Language Tip
Complete the frame "The (text/author) . . ." with a verb that summarizes, such as "emphasizes" or "states." Then add text evidence to support your claim.
For example, "The article emphasizes that a sleep deficit can lead to serious health issues, such as diabetes."

Responding to Evidence
Share your response to data or statistics.

If evidence gets your attention . . .
- One finding that caught my attention is _____.
- A piece of data that caught my attention is that _____.
- One surprising statistic is that _____.

154 Academic Language Handbook

Academic Language Handbook 155

Read the **Language Tips** to help you understand challenging language and how to complete frames with correct grammar.

Choose a **frame** to structure what you say. A **blank line** means that you need to complete the sentence. **Words in parentheses** mean you have a choice of using one of the words or phrases listed.

Requesting Assistance

Ask the teacher or a classmate for help.

If you don't understand what the speaker said . . .

- I couldn't hear you. Could you repeat that?
- I didn't hear you. Please repeat your (idea/response).

If you don't understand what the speaker meant . . .

- I don't quite understand. Could you give me an example?
- I am somewhat confused. Could you explain that again?
- I am not sure I get your point. Could you explain what you mean by _____?

> **Language Tip**
>
> In formal settings, avoid saying "huh?" or "I don't get it" when you don't understand. Instead, politely say, "I am somewhat confused. Could you explain that again?"

Asking for Clarification

Ask for more information.

If you have a question . . .

- I have a question about _____.
- One question I have is _____?

> Will you explain the directions for this assignment again?

If you need information repeated . . .

- Will you explain _____ again?

If you need more explanation . . .

- What do you mean by _____?
- I don't quite understand your (question/suggestion).
- What exactly do you mean by _____?
- Could you explain what you mean by _____?

> What exactly do you mean by "the topic sentence"?

Facilitating Discussion

Collaborate to have a discussion in a small group.

If you want to ask a group member to add an idea . . .

- So _____, what's your (experience/suggestion)?
- So _____, what's your (perspective/point of view)?
- _____, what (reason/example) did you come up with?

If you want to ask a group member about a word . . .

- So _____, are you familiar with the word _____?

If you want to share word knowledge with the group . . .

- No. I have never heard the word _____.
- I'm unfamiliar with the word _____.
- I recognize _____. It has something to do with _____.
- I can use _____ in a sentence. For example, _____.
- I know the word _____. It means _____.

If you want to share word knowledge with the class . . .

- My group members are unfamiliar with the word _____.
- We recognize the word _____, but we would benefit from a review of the meaning.
- We recognize the word _____, but we would benefit from a review of how to use it in a sentence.
- We think _____ means _____.

> No. I have never heard the word "deficit."

Language Tip

Follow "has something to do with . . ." with a noun or verb phrase that you associate with the word.

For example, "I recognize metabolism. It has something to do with your body."

Stating Perspectives

Give your opinion about an issue or a topic.

If you want to share your opinion . . .

- In my (opinion/experience), _____.
- From my (perspective/point of view) _____.
- I know from experience that _____.
- Based on my experience, _____.

> From my perspective, I believe that schools should start later to accommodate teens.

Introducing Evidence

Provide supporting evidence for your claim.

If you want to give text evidence . . .

- For (example/instance), _____.
- To illustrate, _____.
- As an illustration, _____.
- In the text, _____.
- The (text/author) _____.
- In addition, the text _____.
- The data (show/prove) _____.
- (Studies/Recent findings) (show/prove) _____.

Language Tip

Complete the frame "The (text/author) . . ." with a verb that summarizes, such as "emphasizes" or "states." Then add text evidence to support your claim.

For example, "The article emphasizes that a sleep deficit can lead to serious health issues, such as diabetes."

Responding to Evidence

Share your response to data or statistics.

If evidence gets your attention . . .

- One finding that caught my attention is _____.
- A piece of data that caught my attention is that _____.
- One surprising statistic is that _____.

Elaborating

Provide more information and details to support a claim.

If you want to give an example . . .

- For example, _____.
- For instance, _____.
- In particular, _____.
- As an illustration, _____.
- To illustrate, _____.
- To demonstrate, _____.
- In my experience, _____.
- To clarify, _____.
- To exemplify, _____.

> **Language Tip**
>
> "Instance" is a noun that is another way of saying "example." "Exemplify" is a verb that means to give an example.

If you want to share a personal experience . . .

- I know this firsthand because _____.
- I have found that _____.
- I have noticed that _____.
- I have discovered that _____.
- I have observed that _____.
- Based on my experience, _____.
- Personally, _____.

> I know this firsthand because my cousin frequently misses school because he's sleep-deprived.

Restating Ideas

Listen carefully and repeat classmates' ideas in your own words.

If you want to restate someone else's idea . . .

- So you believe that _____.
- So your (opinion/perspective/point of view) is that _____.
- If I understand you correctly, your opinion is that _____.
- So if I understand you correctly, your perspective is that _____.
- In other words, your point of view is that _____.
- In other words, your stance is that _____.

> ### Language Tip
>
> Complete each frame with an independent clause that restates your classmate's idea in your own words.
>
> For example, "So your perspective is that having too many passengers in a car may distract the driver."

If someone restates your idea correctly . . .

- Yes, that's correct.
- Yes, that's accurate.

If someone restates your idea incorrectly . . .

- No, not exactly. What I (pointed out/stated/reported) is _____.
- No, not quite. What I (reported/expressed/suggested) is that _____.
- Actually, what I (suggested/related/specified) is that _____.
- No. What I intended to say is _____.

> Actually, what I specified is that having too many passengers in the car is unsafe.

Agreeing & Disagreeing

Politely tell others if you agree or disagree with their ideas.

I agree with Elena's point of view about raising the minimum driving age.

If you agree with an idea . . .
- I agree with _____'s idea.
- I agree with _____'s opinion.
- I completely agree with _____'s perspective.
- I agree with _____'s point of view about _____.

If you disagree with an idea . . .
- I don't quite agree with _____'s idea.
- I disagree with _____'s opinion.
- I completely disagree with _____'s perspective.
- I disagree with _____'s point of view about _____.

If you are undecided about an idea . . .
- I'm undecided about _____'s idea.
- I'm uncertain about _____'s idea.
- I'm unconvinced about _____'s idea.
- I'm unsure about _____'s idea.
- I see both sides of the issue.
- I can't definitively agree or disagree with _____'s idea.
- I am undecided whether _____.
- I am more inclined to believe that _____.
- I remain unconvinced that _____.
- I need to consider the idea of _____ further.

Language Tip

When you "definitively" agree or disagree with something, your opinion cannot be changed.

Comparing Ideas

Discuss how your ideas are similar to or different from others' ideas.

If your idea is similar . . .

- My (stance/experience/initial reaction) is similar to _____'s.
- My (perspective/point of view) on _____ is similar to _____'s.
- My (idea/initial reaction) is the same.
- _____ and I had similar (experiences/initial reactions).
- My (idea/initial reaction) is related to _____'s.

> ### Language Tip
> Your "stance" on an issue is your position.
>
> Your "initial reaction" is your first thought about something.

If your idea is different . . .

- My (stance/experience/initial reaction) is different from _____'s.
- My (perspective/point of view) on _____ is different from _____'s.
- My (idea/initial reaction) is somewhat different.
- _____ and I had somewhat different (experiences/initial reactions).

> My perspective on requiring world language classes to graduate is different from Jessica's.

Collaborating With Others

Discuss responses with a partner or group members.

If you want to ask a partner or group member to respond . . .

- What should we write?
- What do you think makes sense?
- What do you think works well?
- What do you think fits well?
- What do you think fits logically?
- What do you think is a strong choice?
- What do you think seems reasonable?
- What do you think is a strong selection?
- What do you think works effectively?

If you want to share your response with a partner or group member . . .

- We could put _____.
- We could also write _____.
- We could choose _____.
- Another option is _____.
- Another possibility is _____.
- In addition, we could write _____.
- We could select _____.
- Additionally, we could write _____.
- As an alternative, we could write _____.
- Alternatively, we could write _____.

As an alternative, we could write the word "exhausted."

Reporting Ideas

Share ideas during a class discussion.

If you are reporting responses . . .

- We thought of _____.
- We came up with _____.
- We chose _____.
- We decided upon _____.
- We agreed upon _____.
- We selected _____.
- We opted for _____.
- We came to a consensus on _____.

If you are choosing precise words . . .

- We would like to (suggest/recommend/propose) the precise word _____.
- We (decided/agreed) upon the precise word

  _____.
- We selected the precise word _____.
- We opted for the precise word _____.
- We came to a consensus on the precise word _____.
- One precise word we (identified/considered/proposed) is _____.
- One precise word we (decided/agreed) upon is

  _____.
- One precise word we selected is _____.
- One precise word we opted for is _____.
- One precise word we came to a consensus on is _____.

> We would like to propose the precise word "lethargic."

Language Tip

When you "come to a consensus" with your group members, it means that you all agree on the response.

Summarizing

State the key ideas and details of a text.

A central idea in this text is that knowing another language is beneficial when applying for jobs.

If you want to state the key idea . . .

- The key idea of this text is _____.
- The author's main idea is _____.
- This text is mainly about _____.
- The text is primarily about _____.
- This text focuses on _____.
- A central idea in this text is _____.

If you want to describe key details . . .

- (One/Another) important detail is _____.
- (One/Another) key detail in this text is _____.
- (One/An additional) essential detail is _____.
- (One/An additional) significant detail is _____.
- (One/An additional) relevant supporting detail in this text is _____.
- Perhaps the most (important/significant/relevant) detail in this text is _____.

Language Tip

Choose a precise adjective that fits the detail you describe:

- An "essential" detail proves a point or supports a topic.
- A "significant" detail has an important influence or effect on the topic or issue.
- A "relevant" detail is related to your position.

Paraphrasing

Restate and explain an author's ideas in your own words.

If you want to restate an author's idea . . .

- To put it another way, _____.
- To paraphrase, _____.
- In other words, _____.
- In this quote, the author states _____.
- In this quote, the author makes a case for _____.

If you want to explain what an author means . . .

- This quote reinforces the idea that _____.
- This quote clarifies that _____.
- The author seems to be saying that _____.
- This quote makes it evident that _____.

Language Tip

Paraphrase text evidence that supports your claim when you write a justification or argument.

For example, "In other words, teaching practical skills in high school helps prepare students for their future careers."

This quote reinforces the idea that raising the driving age would inconvenience parents.

Affirming Ideas

Acknowledge a classmate's idea before stating your own idea.

If you want to acknowledge others' ideas . . .

- That's an interesting claim.
- I hadn't thought of that.
- That's an interesting opinion.
- I see what you mean.
- I can understand why you see it this way.
- That's an intriguing perspective.
- That's a compelling stance.
- That's a thought-provoking point of view.

In my opinion, teens should have credit cards so that they learn how to be responsible and manage their money.

I hadn't thought of that.

Offering Feedback

Share your feedback and suggestions about a classmate's writing or speech.

If you want to give positive feedback . . .

- You did an effective job of organizing _____.
- You did an effective job of including _____.
- You did an effective job of stating _____.
- I appreciate how you used _____.
- I appreciate how you included _____.
- I appreciate your effort to (organize/include/ state) _____.
- I appreciate your use of _____.
- I appreciate your skillful _____.

If you want to offer a suggestion . . .

- Your (writing/speech) _____ would be stronger if you _____.
- As you revise your (writing/speech) _____, focus on _____.
- As you revise your (writing/speech) _____, make a point of _____.

> ### Language Tip
>
> Complete the frames with a noun phrase to give positive feedback.
>
> For example, "You did an effective job of stating reasons why you think a second language should be a requirement to graduate."

As you revise your argument, make a point of including relevant text evidence to support your claim.

WORD ANALYSIS

Vocabulary to Analyze Context

Teach students these technical terms to competently engage in analyzing context and word parts as clues to word meaning.

analyze

verb to carefully examine something to understand it.

analysis

noun a careful examination of something to understand it.

context

noun the language surrounding a word or phrase that helps you understand it.

prefix

noun a group of letters added to the beginning of a word to change its meaning.

mis + *understand* = *misunderstand*

suffix

noun a letter or group of letters added to the end of a word that changes the part of speech.

polite (adjective) + *ness* = *politeness (noun)*

root word

noun a word that is used as a base to create other words by adding a prefix or suffix, often coming from Greek or Latin.

un + *think* + *able* = *unthinkable*

Common Prefixes & Suffixes

Learn these affixes to use as clues to the meanings of unfamiliar words.

Prefix	Meaning	Example Words
anti–	against	antiperspirant, antisocial
dis–	not, opposite of	disagree, disapprove
im–, in–	not	immature, insignificant
inter–	between	international, interactive
mis–	bad, wrong	miscalculate, misunderstand
non–, un–	not	nonviolence, unauthorized, unsupervised
pre–	before	prepay, precede
re–	again	reread, reconsider
sub–	below, under	subconscious, subtitle
trans–	across	transaction, transport

Suffix	Meaning	Example Words
–able, –ible *(adj)*	having a particular quality; something that is possible	comparable, valuable, accessible
–ate *(verb)*	to make, cause, or act	accumulate, communicate, regulate
–ation, –ion *(noun)*	the act or result of doing something	preparation, innovation, contribution, determination
–er, –or *(noun)*	someone who does	manager, organizer, investigator, mentor
–ful *(adj)*	full of	doubtful, harmful
–ity *(noun)*	having a particular quality	capacity, identity, productivity
–ive *(adj)*	having a particular quality	collaborative, productive, representative
–less *(adj)*	without	careless, powerless
–ly *(adv)*	to happen in a particular way	accurately, certainly, simultaneously
–ment *(noun)*	the result	achievement, enforcement, investment, requirement

ACADEMIC GLOSSARY

A glossary is a useful tool found at the back of many books. It contains information about key words in the text. Review the sample glossary entry below.

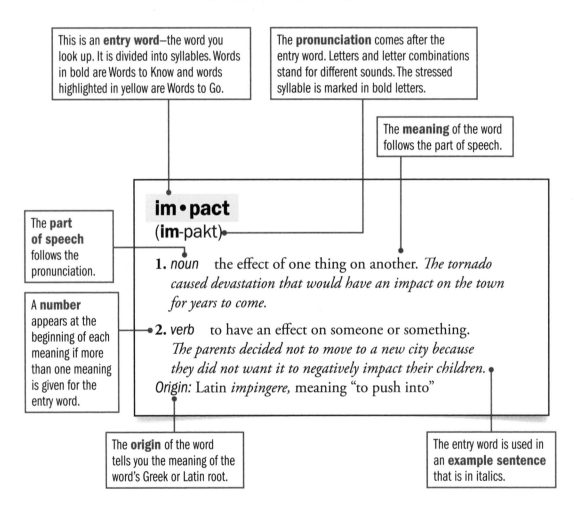

This is an **entry word**—the word you look up. It is divided into syllables. Words in bold are Words to Know and words highlighted in yellow are Words to Go.

The **pronunciation** comes after the entry word. Letters and letter combinations stand for different sounds. The stressed syllable is marked in bold letters.

The **meaning** of the word follows the part of speech.

The **part of speech** follows the pronunciation.

A **number** appears at the beginning of each meaning if more than one meaning is given for the entry word.

im•pact
(**im**-pakt)

1. *noun*   the effect of one thing on another. *The tornado caused devastation that would have an impact on the town for years to come.*

2. *verb*   to have an effect on someone or something. *The parents decided not to move to a new city because they did not want it to negatively impact their children.*
Origin: Latin *impingere,* meaning "to push into"

The **origin** of the word tells you the meaning of the word's Greek or Latin root.

The entry word is used in an **example sentence** that is in italics.

ac•cess
(**ak**-ses)

verb to find/get information, especially on a computer. *Only someone with the correct password can access the computer files.*

Origin: Latin *accedere*, meaning "to approach"

ac•ces•si•ble
(**ak**-ses-si-buhl)

adjective able to find/get information. *The computer files became accessible once I entered the correct password.*

Origin: Latin *accedere*, meaning "to approach"

ac•com•mo•date
(uh-**kah**-muh-date)

verb to have enough space for a particular number of people or things. *The field was large enough to accommodate the entire team.*

Origin: Latin *accommodare*, meaning "make fit"

ac•com•mo•da•tion
(uh-kah-muh-**day**-shuhn)

noun a place for someone to stay, live, or work. *My neighbors found accommodation for the family who had lost their home in the fire.*

Origin: Latin *accommodare*, meaning "make fit"

ac•count•a•ble
(uh-**kount**-ah-buhl)

adjective responsible for the effects of your actions and willing to explain them. *The mayor met with business owners because she is accountable to the people who live in her city.*

ac•cu•mu•late
(uh-**kyoo**-myuh-late)

verb to increase gradually in numbers or amount until there is a large quantity. *Jesse accumulated 50 participation points this semester in freshman English for his voluntary contributions during class discussions.*

Origin: Latin *accumulare*, meaning "to heap"

ac•cu•rate•ly
(**ak**-yuh-ruht-lee)

adverb in a way that is correct and true in every detail. *The experiment required all students to measure accurately in order to get the best results.*

Origin: Latin *accuratus*, meaning "done with care"

a•chieve
(uh-**cheev**)

verb to succeed in accomplishing the result you want. *The team worked hard to achieve the title of state champions.*

a•chieve•ment
(uh-**cheev**-muhnt)

noun an important result that is gained by effort. *Getting an A in biology was a big achievement, since the class was so difficult.*

ac•knowl•edge
(ak-**nah**-lij)

verb to accept or admit the truth about something. *The parents were proud when their daughter chose to acknowledge she had made a mistake.*

ACADEMIC GLOSSARY

ac•quire
(uh-**kwire**)

verb   to gain or learn something. *Many long practices helped the team members acquire the skills they needed to work together.*

Origin: Latin *acquirere,* meaning "get in addition"

ac•qui•si•tion
(ak-wuh-**zi**-shuhn)

noun   the process by which someone gains or learns something. *The acquisition of my CD collection has taken several years.*

Origin: Latin *acquirere,* meaning "get in addition"

a•dapt
(uh-**dapt**)

verb   to change so that you can succeed in a different situation. *On the first day of school the new student had to adapt to his surroundings.*

Origin: Latin *adaptare,* meaning "to fit"

ad•mis•sion
(ad-**mi**-shuhn)

noun   the process someone goes through to join a club, school, or group. *You have to attend tryouts if you want to gain admission to the school band.*

Origin: Latin *admittere,* meaning "to send"

ad•mit
(ad-**mit**)

verb   to let someone join a club, school, event, or group. *Because the venue was full, the concert organizers would not admit anyone else.*

Origin: Latin *admittere,* meaning "to send"

ad•o•les•cence
(ad-uh-**less**-uhnss)

noun   the period of time when a young person becomes an adult; teenager. *Adolescence is a time when a person's body goes through many changes.*

Origin: Latin *adolescere,* meaning "grow to maturity"

ad•o•les•cent
(ad-uh-**less**-uhnt)

noun   a young person who is becoming an adult; teenager. *An adolescent does not usually like the same kind of music as his or her parents.*

Origin: Latin *adolescent-,* meaning "coming to maturity"

ad•van•tage
(uhd-**van**-tij)

noun   something that helps you to be better or more successful; something that is good or useful about a place, thing, or situation. *One advantage of being tall is the ability to reach items in high places.*

Origin: Latin *abante,* meaning "in front"

ad•vo•cate
(**ad**-vuh-kate)

1. *verb*   to support or recommend an idea or plan. *The principal felt strongly about the need to advocate the importance of education.*

(**ad**-vuh-kit)

2. *noun*   a person who publicly supports an idea or plan. *My brother is an advocate for developing a fire safety plan for our family.*

Origin: Latin *advocare,* meaning "to call (to one's aid)"

af•fect
(uh-**fekt**)

verb   to change someone or something.
No one expected the storm to affect our neighborhood to such an extent.

Origin: Latin *afficere*, meaning "produce an effect on, influence"

al•ter•na•tive
(awl-**tur**-nuh-tiv)

noun   something you can choose instead of something else. *Unlike the first solution, the alternative satisfied everyone.*

Origin: Latin *alternare*, meaning "interchange"

a•non•y•mi•ty
(an-uh-**nim**-i-tee)

noun   when other people do not know who you are or what your name is. *The new student's anonymity did not last long once she began making friends.*

Origin: Greek *anōnumos*, meaning "nameless"

a•non•y•mous
(uh-**nah**-nuh-muhs)

adjective   describing a person who is not identified by name. *The money from the anonymous donor helped the school buy new books.*

Origin: Greek *anōnumos*, meaning "nameless"

ap•par•ent
(uh-**par**-uhnt)

adjective   easily noticed. *The winning team's exhaustion was apparent.*

Origin: Latin *apparent-*, meaning "appearing"

ap•proach
(uh-**prohch**)

noun   a way of doing something. *The first solution didn't work, so I tried a new approach.*

Origin: Latin *appropriare*, meaning "draw near"

ar•ray
(uh-**ray**)

1. *noun*   a collection of things that are related in some way. *She was excited by the array of prom dresses in the store.*

2. *verb*   to arrange something in an attractive way. *The teacher will array the student paintings in the showcase.*

as•pect
(**as**-pekt)

noun   one feature or characteristic of something that has more than one feature or characteristic. *Bonding with my teammates is the most enjoyable aspect of being on the soccer team.*

Origin: Latin *aspectus*, meaning "look at"

as•sist
(uh-**sist**)

verb   to help someone do something. *The student interns assist on the set of the television show.*

Origin: Latin *assistere*, meaning "defend"

as•sure
(uh-**shoor**)

verb   to tell someone that something will definitely happen so that they are less worried. *I can assure you that I will arrive by eight o'clock in the morning.*

Origin: Latin *assecurare*, meaning "to make secure with pledge or promise"

ACADEMIC GLOSSARY

at·trib·u·ta·ble
(uh-**trib**-yoot-uh-buhl)

adjective   likely to have been caused by something. *The success of the fundraiser was attributable to the preparation done beforehand.*

Origin: Latin *attribuere*, meaning "to bestow or pay"

at·trib·ute
(uh-**trib**-yoot)

verb   to give someone or something credit. *The boy felt he could attribute his good grades to his many hours of studying.*

Origin: Latin *attribuere*, meaning "to bestow or pay"

bal·ance
(**bal**-uhns)

noun   the remaining amount of money that is still owed. *After paying part of the bill, Kyle still owed a balance of $20.*

Origin: Latin *bilanx*, meaning "having two plates (as on a scale)"

ban
(**ban**)

1. *verb*   to not allow something to be done, seen, used, etc. *The teachers wanted to ban the use of cell phones during class.*

2. *noun*   a rule made that does not allow something to be done, seen, used, etc. *The principal placed a ban on using cell phones in class.*

bank·rupt
(**bangk**-ruhpt)

adjective   without enough money to pay what is owed. *The restaurant did not make enough money, so it went bankrupt.*

bank·rupt·cy
(**bangk**-ruhpt-see)

noun   the state of being without enough money to pay what is owed. *The employees were surprised to learn their company was facing bankruptcy.*

bar·ri·er
(**ba**-ree-ur)

noun   a rule or a problem that prevents or limits people from doing something. *The speed limit is a barrier against driving too fast.*

ben·e·fi·cial
(ben-uh-**fish**-uhl)

adjective   having a good or helpful effect. *Study hall can be beneficial for students who do not have time to do homework after school.*

Origin: Latin *beneficium*, meaning "help"

ben·e·fit
(**ben**-uh-fit)

noun   something that is helpful or good for you. *One benefit to study hall is being able to finish your homework before leaving school.*

Origin: Latin *benefactum*, meaning "good deed"

bi·as
(bi-**uhs**)

noun   an opinion about whether a person, group, or idea is good or bad. *The unfair calls made us think the referee had a bias against our team.*

bi•lin•gual
(bye-**ling**-gwuhl)

adjective   speaking two languages equally well. *My parents grew up in Mexico and are bilingual in Spanish and English.*

Origin: Latin *bilinguis*, meaning "having two tongues"

bi•lin•gual•is•m
(bye-**ling**-gwuhl-iz-uhm)

noun   the ability to speak two languages equally well. *Bilingualism is common among people who spend time in different countries.*

Origin: Latin *bilinguis*, meaning "having two tongues"

ca•pac•i•ty
(kuh-**pass**-i-tee)

noun   the mental or physical ability to do or learn something. *Will is an actor with a capacity for memorizing lots of dialogue.*

Origin: Latin *capacitas*, meaning "ability"

cer•ti•fied
(**sur**-ti-fyed)

adjective   having successfully completed a training course for a particular profession. *Some teachers must pass a state test to become certified.*

Origin: Latin *certus*, meaning "certain"

chal•lenge
(**chal**-inj)

noun difficult but also interesting or enjoyable. *When I first started playing saxophone, it was a challenge just to play a note.*

chal•leng•ing
(**chal**-inj-ing)

adjective difficult but also interesting or enjoyable to accomplish. *The team met the challenging goal of reaching the state finals.*

cit•i•zen
(**sit**-i-zuhn)

noun   a person who has responsibilities as well as full rights in a particular country or place. *If you are born in the United States, you are an American citizen.*

Origin: Latin *civitas*, meaning "city"

cit•i•zen•ship
(**sit**-uh-zuhn-ship)

noun   the full rights in a particular country or place. *One way to gain citizenship in the United States is to pass a test about the country.*

Origin: Latin *civitas*, meaning "city"

civ•ic
(**siv**-ik)

adjective   of or having to do with a city or the people who live there. *It is the civic duty of everyone who lives in this town to throw away their trash.*

Origin: Latin *civicus*, meaning "citizen"

cog•ni•tive
(**kog**-nuh-tiv)

adjective   relating to activities of the mind, such as thinking. *I love difficult riddles because they exercise my cognitive skills.*

Origin: Latin *cognitivus*, meaning "known"

col•lab•o•ra•tive
(kuh-**lab**-uh-ra-tiv)

adjective   able to work closely with others to achieve something. *The collaborative efforts of everyone helped to finish the project quickly.*

Origin: Latin *collaborare*, meaning "to work together"

com•mod•i•ty
(kuh-**mah**-di-tee)

noun   a useful quality. *More time to sleep is a commodity that many people would like in their lives.*

Origin: Latin *commodus*, meaning "convenient"

com•mu•ni•cate
(kuh-**myoo**-nuh-kate)

verb   to share information or ideas with others. *It is helpful to communicate with others when trying to solve a problem.*

Origin: Latin *communicat-*, meaning "shared"

com•mu•ni•ca•tion
(kuh-**myoo**-nuh-kay-shuhn)

noun   the act of sharing information or expressing thoughts and feelings. *Both siblings admitted they were wrong, and this honest communication ended the argument.*

Origin: Latin *communicat-*, meaning "shared"

com•pa•ra•ble
(kuhm-**par**-uh-buhl)

adjective   similar to something else in size, number, quality, etc. *Although the two dogs were different breeds, they were comparable in size.*

Origin: Latin *comparare*, meaning "equal"

com•pen•sate
(**kahm**-puhn-sate)

verb   to pay or make up for something. *The plants need extra watering to compensate for the lack of rain.*

Origin: Latin *compensat-*, meaning "balance"

com•pe•tent
(**kahm**-puh-tuhnt)

adjective   having enough skill or knowledge to do something well. *Because she practiced so often, Jade quickly became competent at playing the piano.*

Origin: Latin *competere*, meaning "suitable, appropriate"

com•pe•ti•tion
(kahm-puh-**tish**-uhn)

noun   a task, game, or contest in which there is a winner. *Julio was the only undefeated player in the competition.*

Origin: Latin *competitio*, meaning "rivalry"

com•pet•i•tive
(kuhm-**pet**-i-tiv)

adjective   as good as or better than others at a job, task, or contest. *Alexa practiced hard so that she would be competitive with the other girls trying out for the team.*

Origin: Latin *competit-*, meaning "striven for"

com • pla • cent
(kuhm-**play**-suhnt)

adjective   pleased with a situation enough to stop trying to change or improve things. *The smartest students do not become complacent just because they get good grades.*

Origin: Latin *complacent-*, meaning "pleasing"

com • plex
(kuhm-**pleks** or **kahm**-pleks)

adjective   having many parts or details and often difficult to understand. *The complex math problem required extra time to solve.*

Origin: Latin *complectere*, meaning "embrace, grasp"

com • pre • hen • sive
(kahm-pre-**hen**-siv)

adjective   including everything that is necessary. *The comprehensive exam included everything that we had learned in class that year.*

Origin: Latin *comprehendere*, meaning "to catch or take hold"

con • duct
(kuhn-**duhkt**)

verb   to carry out an activity or process, especially to get information or prove facts. *If the missing book is not located, the library will have to conduct a search for it.*

Origin: Latin *conducere*, meaning "to lead or bring together"

con • flict
(**kahn**-flict)

noun   a situation in which people do not agree. *The new list of chores created conflict between my siblings and my parents.*

Origin: Latin *confligere*, meaning "argue or clash"

con • front
(kuhn-**fruhnt**)

verb   to deal with a problem; appear and cause problems. *It is time that we confront the bullying problem at our school and do something to fix it.*

Origin: Latin *confrontare*, meaning "with (a person's) face"

con • sen • sus
(kuhn-**sen**-suhs)

noun   an agreement among all the people in a group. *The group consensus was to go to the park instead of the movies.*

Origin: Latin *consentire*, meaning "agreement"

con • se • quence
(**kahn**-suh-kwens)

noun   something that happens because of an action. *Punishment is a consequence of not following the rules.*

Origin: Latin *consequentia*, meaning "following closely"

ACADEMIC GLOSSARY

con•sid•er
(kuhn-**sid**-ur)
verb   to think about something carefully; to have an opinion about someone or something. *You should consider all your options before deciding which movie to see.*
Origin: Latin *considerare*, meaning "examine"

con•sti•tu•tion•al
(kahn-stuh-**too**-shuhn-uhl)
adjective   of or relating to the written document containing the basic laws. *Freedom of speech is a constitutional right.*
Origin: Latin *constitutio*, meaning "arrangement"

con•tri•bute
(kuhn-**trib**-yoot)
verb   to give or do something to help make something successful. *Everyone must contribute in order to make our project successful.*
Origin: Latin *contribut-*, meaning "brought together, added"

con•tri•bu•ting
(kuhn-**tri**-byoo-ting)
adjective   helping to make something happen. *One contributing factor in the gymnast's success is the support of her coach.*
Origin: Latin *contribut-*, meaning "brought together, added"

con•tri•bu•tion
(kahn-tri-**byoo**-shuhn)
noun   something that a person gives or does to help something be successful. *Our family's contribution helped the fundraisers reach their goal.*
Origin: Latin *contribuere*, meaning "bring together, add"

con•ven•tion•al
(kuhn-**ven**-shuh-nuhl)
adjective   around for a long time; considered to be usual or traditional. *Conventional letters are being replaced by emails and texts.*
Origin: Latin *conventionalis*, meaning "meeting"

cred•it
(**kred**-it)
noun   an agreement that allows you to buy something and pay for it later. *Chloe bought the car with credit and will pay it off over time.*
Origin: Latin *creditum*, meaning "trust"

crit•i•cal
(**krit**-i-kuhl)
adjective   very important, because what happens in the future depends on it. *It is critical that we buy supplies before the storm.*
Origin: Latin *criticus* and Greek *kritikos*, meaning "judge, decide"

crit•i•cism
(**krit**-i-siz-uhm)
noun   remarks that say what you think is bad about someone or something. *The musician received some criticism over the content of his song lyrics.*
Origin: Latin *criticus* and Greek *kritikos*, meaning "judge, decide"

crit•i•cize
(**krit**-i-size)

verb   to express strong disapproval or dislike of a person, idea, or organization. *My parents criticize my brother for his messy room.*
Origin: Latin *criticus* and Greek *kritikos*, meaning "judge, decide"

crit•ics
(**krit**-iks)

noun   people who express strong disapproval or dislike of a person, idea, or organization. *Critics of eliminating foreign language instruction spoke at the meeting.*
Origin: Latin *criticus* and Greek *kritikos*, meaning "judge, decide"

cru•cial
(**kroo**-shuhl)

adjective   something that is extremely important. *Doing well on tomorrow's exam is crucial if you want to pass this class.*
Origin: Latin *crux-*, *curc-*, meaning "cross"

cul•tur•al
(kuhl-chur-uhl)

adjective   having to do with the art, ideas, and beliefs of a group of people. *Lindsey noticed many cultural differences between her hometown and her new neighborhood.*
Origin: Latin *cultura*, meaning "growing, caring for plants or crops"

cul•ture
(**kuhl**-chur)

noun   the way of life shared by people in a particular place or society. *My neighborhood's culture is very different today than it was when my parents were young.*
Origin: Latin *cultura*, meaning "growing, caring for plants or crops"

cyn•i•cism
(**sin**-uh-siz-uhm)

noun   a belief that people do not have good, honest, or sincere reasons for doing something. *The positive actions of the new town council have reduced cynicism in the community.*

da•ta
(**day**-tuh)

noun   information or facts. *The scientists collected data to help prove their theory.*
Origin: Latin *datum*, meaning "something given"

debt
(**det**)

noun   money or something else that is borrowed and should be paid back. *Callie was in debt to her brother after borrowing money from him.*
Origin: Latin *debitum*, meaning "something that is owed"

de•cline
(di-**kline**)

1. *verb*   to decrease in quantity or importance. *Sales of music CDs will continue to decline because people now download music from the Internet.*
2. *noun*   a gradual decrease in the quality, quantity, or importance of something. *The store closed because of a decline in sales.*
Origin: Latin *declinare*, meaning "bend downward, turn aside"

de•clin•ing
(di-**kline**-ing)

verb decreasing in quantity or importance. *The school's population is declining because families are moving to a different neighborhood.*

Origin: Latin *declinare*, meaning "bend downward, turn aside"

def•i•cit
(**def**-i-sit)

noun the difference between how much you have and how much you need. *Tim got a second job to help eliminate the deficit between his savings and the cost of the laptop.*

Origin: Latin *deficit*, meaning "it is lacking"

de•lib•er•ate•ly
(duh-**lib**-ur-it-lee)

adverb done in a way that is planned or intended. *My sister deliberately ruined her sneakers so she could get new ones.*

Origin: Latin *deliberatus*, meaning "considered carefully"

de•moc•ra•cy
(di-**mah**-kruh-see)

noun a system of government where the people choose their leaders. *The United States is a democracy because the people vote to select their president.*

Origin: Greek *dēmos*, meaning "the people," + *kratia*, meaning "power, rule"

dem•o•crat•ic
(dem-uh-**krat**-ik)

adjective referring to the idea that everyone should be involved in making decisions. *The team leader felt that a democratic vote would be the best way to make the decision.*

Origin: Greek *dēmos*, meaning "the people," + *kratia*, meaning "power, rule"

dem•on•strate
(**dem**-uhn-strate)

verb to protest or support something at a public event. *The crowd gathered to demonstrate against the planned removal of the community playground.*

Origin: Latin *demonstrat-*, meaning "pointed out"

dem•on•stra•tion
(dem-uhn-**stray**-shuhn)

noun a protest or public gathering to support something. *The demonstration in support of the new park brought the community closer together.*

Origin: Latin *demonstrate(n-)*, meaning "point out"

de•spite
(di-**spite**)

preposition when something happens even though something else may have prevented it. *The marathon runner broke a record despite the intense heat.*

de•ter•mi•na•tion
(di-**tur**-mi-nay-shuhn)

noun the strong desire/intention to do something and not let anything or anyone stop you. *You could see the determination in the runner's eyes as she crossed the finish line.*

Origin: Latin *determinare*, meaning "limit, fix"

de•ter•mined
(di-**tur**-mihnd)

adjective having a strong desire to do something and not letting anything stop you. *Alli was determined to do well on the test, so she asked her teacher for extra help.*

Origin: Latin *determinare*, meaning "limit, fix"

de•vote
(di-**voht**)

verb   to use all or most of your time, money, or attention to do something or help someone. *The teacher will devote more time to working with individual students.*

Origin: Latin *devotus*, meaning "promised"

dif•fer•en•ti•ate
(dif-ur-**en**-she-ate)

verb   to identify ways in which two or more things or people are not alike. *Colleges look for students who can differentiate themselves from the crowd.*

Origin: Latin *differentia*, meaning "difference"

dig•it•al
(**dij**-i-tuhl)

adjective   involving or relating to the use of electronic or computer technology. *There is a growing demand for digital books.*

Origin: Latin *digitalis*, meaning "finger, toe"

di•min•ish
(duh-**min**-ish)

verb   to become smaller or less important. *Having a dog at home to keep her company may diminish her feelings of loneliness.*

Origin: Latin *deminuere*, meaning "lessen"

dis•ci•pline
(**dis**-uh-plin)

noun   the ability to control your own or someone else's behavior. *It takes a lot of discipline to stay calm when you are really angry about something.*

Origin: Latin *disciplina*, meaning "instruction, knowledge"

dis•tin•guish be•tween
(dis-**ting**-gwish bi-tween)

verb   to tell the difference between two things. *It can be difficult to distinguish between two similar ringtones.*

Origin: Latin *distinguere*, meaning "apart, put out"

dis•tract•ed
(di-**strakt**-ed)

adjective   unable to focus on what you are doing. *Armando acted in a distracted way due to his brother's loud music.*

Origin: Latin *distrahere*, meaning "drawn apart"

dis•trac•tion
(di-**strakt**-shuhn)

noun   something that takes your attention away from what you are doing. *The distraction of the loud TV show kept Emily from getting her work done.*

Origin: Latin *distrahere*, meaning "drawn apart"

du•ty
(**doo**-tee)

noun   a thing a person must do because it is morally or legally right. *The girl felt it was her duty to return the lost wallet she found on the bus.*

dy•nam•ic
(dye-**nam**-ik)

adjective   constantly changing due to many influences. *I get bored easily, so I need to look for a job in a dynamic industry like technology.*

Origin: Greek *dynamikos*, meaning "power"

ACADEMIC GLOSSARY

ef•fec•tive
(i-**fek**-tiv)
adjective   having the intended result. *An effective study routine can help students reach their academic goals.*
Origin: Latin *effectivus*, meaning "accomplish"

ef•fect•ive•ness
(i-**fek**-tiv-ness)
noun   power to bring about the intended result; success. *Mr. William's effectiveness as head coach was proven when the track team won all their meets.*
Origin: Latin *effectivus*, meaning "accomplish"

e•lim•i•nate
(i-**lim**-uh-nate)
verb   to completely get rid of an unnecessary or unwanted item. *Natasha had to eliminate peanuts from her diet after she discovered she was allergic to them.*
Origin: Latin *eliminare*, meaning "send outdoors"

em•pha•sis
(**em**-fuh-siss)
noun   importance put on something. *The coach placed emphasis on teamwork rather than on winning.*
Origin: Greek *emphainein*, meaning "exhibit"

em•pha•size
(**em**-fuh-size)
verb   to draw attention to something. *My parents emphasize the importance of seat belts whenever we get in the car.*
Origin: Greek *emphainein*, meaning "exhibit"

en•a•ble
(en-**ay**-buhl)
verb   to make it possible for someone to do something. *Flashlights enable us to see in the dark.*

en•force
(en-**fors**)
verb   to make sure that a law or rule is obeyed. *It is a police officer's job to enforce traffic laws.*

en•force•ment
(en-**fors**-muhnt)
noun   the act of making people obey a rule or law. *The principal began the enforcement of a new dress code for students.*

en•hance
(en-**hans**)
verb   to improve something. *I was able to enhance the colors in my grandparents' wedding photo using my new computer program.*
Origin: Latin *inaltare*, meaning "raise"

en•hanced
(en-**hansd**)

adjective   improved or better. *The enhanced version of the DVD contains a lot of special features.*

Origin: Latin *inaltare*, meaning "raise"

en•vi•ron•ment
(en-**vye**-ruhn-muhnt)

noun   the people and things that surround and affect someone. *My three younger siblings can make my house a very noisy environment!*

en•vi•ron•ment•al
(en-vye-ruhn-**mehn**-tuhl)

adjective   concerning the people and things around someone. *Pollution can cause an environmental threat to wildlife and people.*

e•quiv•a•lent
(i-**kwiv**-uh-luhnt)

1. *noun*   something that has the same value, size, or purpose as something else. *Workers in some poor countries earn the equivalent of three dollars a day.*

2. *adjective*   equal in value to something or someone else. *A pint of liquid is equivalent to two cups.*

Origin: Latin *aequivalent-*, meaning "being of equal worth"

es•tab•lish
(i-**stab**-lish)

verb   to start up something that will last for some time. *It did not take the local deli long to establish itself in the neighborhood.*

Origin: Latin *stabilire*, meaning "make firm"

es•tab•lish•ing
(i-**stab**-lish-ing)

verb   making people accept that you can do something. *The doctor's research is establishing her as an expert in her field.*

Origin: Latin *stabilire*, meaning "make firm"

es•tab•lish•ment
(i-**stab**-lish-muhnt)

noun   the people who are in control of a society or profession. *The political establishment was resistant to the changes some voters wanted them to make.*

Origin: Latin *stabilire*, meaning "make firm"

es•ti•mate
(**es**-tuh-muht)

noun   a rough guess about an amount, distance, value, or other quantity. *The driver calculated an estimate of how many hours the trip would take.*

Origin: Latin *aestimat-*, meaning "determined, appraised"

es•ti•mat•ed
(**es**-tuh-mate-ed)

adjective   roughly calculated in a way that is not exact. *It took an estimated 20 hours to build the sandcastle.*

Origin: Latin *aestimat-*, meaning "determined, appraised"

e•val•u•ate
(i-**val**-yoo-ate)

verb   to decide how good or useful something is. *Many companies evaluate how well a product will sell before putting it in stores.*

e•volve
(i-**vahlv**)

verb to change slowly over a long period of time. *Technology needs to evolve to meet the growing demand for fast communication.*

Origin: Latin *evolvere*, meaning "to unroll"

ex•pe•ri•ence
(ik-**speer**-ee-uhns)

noun the skill or knowledge someone has because they have done something for a long time. *Leo's previous work experience helped him get a new job.*

Origin: Latin *experientia*, meaning "try"

ex•pe•ri•enced
(ik-**speer**-ee-uhnsd)

adjective having skills or knowledge because you have done something for a long time. *The experienced skater could skate backward without falling.*

Origin: Latin *experientia*, meaning "try"

ex•per•tise
(ek-spur-**teez**)

noun special skills or knowledge developed in a particular subject. *After graduating college, the students looked for jobs that would fit their expertise.*

ex•tro•vert•ed
(**ek**-struh-vurt-ed)

adjective confident and enjoying being with other people. *The extroverted teenager always organizes activities for her and her friends to do.*

Origin: Latin *extro-,* meaning "outside," + *vertere,* meaning "to turn"

fac•tor
(**fak**-tur)

noun one of the things that causes a result. *The weather will be one factor in deciding whether or not to cancel the game.*

Origin: Latin *factor*, meaning "doer or maker"

fee
(fee)

noun the amount of money charged for a service. *Depending on the size of the project, the contractor's fee will change.*

field
(**feeld**)

noun a person's area of interest, or a subject of study. *I do not like the sight of blood, so I do not plan on working in the medical field.*

fi•nan•ces
(**fye**-nan-ses)

noun the amount of money a person or company has. *My mom is in charge of managing our family's finances.*

fi•nan•cial
(fye-**nan**-shuhl)

adjective relating to the management and use of money. *My brother was able to get out of debt once he developed a stronger financial plan.*

fix•ed
(fiksd)

adjective not changing or able to be changed. *The math equation must be solved in a fixed order.*

Origin: Latin *fixare*, meaning "to unroll"

fo•cus
(**foh**-kuhs)

verb to give special attention to something or somebody. *It is important to focus when you read so that you will be able to answer questions about the text later.*

gen•er•a•tion
(jen-uh-**ray**-shuhn)

noun all the people who are about the same age. *Grandchildren are the younger generation in a family.*

Origin: Latin *gernerat-*, meaning "created"

glob•al
(**gloh**-buhl)

adjective affecting or involving the whole world. *The global use of technology means we often communicate in a similar way worldwide.*

glob•al•i•za•tion
(gloh-buhl-i-**zay**-shuhn)

noun the process of something becoming present all over the world. *The globalization of some restaurant chains means that you can get the same kind of food wherever you are.*

grit
(**grit**)

noun courage or determination shown in a difficult situation. *Although he was exhausted, Michael showed grit and finished the race.*

hor•mone
(**hor**-mone)

noun a chemical in the body that affects how it grows and develops. *In the adolescent years, a person's levels of hormones begin to change.*

Origin: Greek *horman*, meaning "stir up"

hy•po•crites
(**hip**-uh-krits)

noun people whose behavior or statements show that their beliefs and the things they say are not sincere. *If the senators do not pass the crime bill they said they would support, they will be hypocrites.*

i•den•ti•ty
(eye-**den**-ti-tee)

noun a sense of self; a feeling of belonging to a particular group or race. *Culture, family, and friends all influence a person's identity.*

Origin: Latin *identitas*, meaning "same"

i•de•o•log•i•cal
(eye-dee-oh-**loj**-i-kal)

adjective based on a particular set of beliefs or ideas. *The two politicians had different views, so they often argued about ideological differences.*

Origin: Greek *idea*, meaning "form, pattern," + *–logos*, meaning "word, speech, discourse"

im•ma•ture
(im-uh-**choor** or im-uh-**toor**)

adjective   not fully grown or developed; to act younger than your age. *The immature seedling is not yet ready to be planted.*

Origin: Latin *immaturus*, meaning "untimely, unripe"

im•pact
(**im**-pakt)

1. *noun*   the effect of one thing on another. *The tornado caused devastation that would have an impact on the town for years to come.*

2. *verb*   to have an effect on someone or something. *The parents decided not to move to a new city because they did not want it to negatively impact their children.*

Origin: Latin *impingere*, meaning "to push into"

im•pet•u•ous
(im-**pech**-oo-uhs)

adjective   tending to do things quickly without thinking carefully first. *Someone who acts without thinking may need to be less impetuous.*

Origin: Latin *impetuosus*, meaning "to attack"

im•pose
(im-**poze**)

verb   to force people to accept a rule, punishment, tax, etc. *My mom does not impose the same rules on me as she does on my baby brother.*

Origin: Latin *imponere*, meaning "inflict, deceive"

im•pulse
(**im**-puhls)

noun   the urge to act without thinking about the possible results or dangers. *Being friends with Emma is unpredictable because you never know what impulse will strike her next.*

Origin: Latin *impuls-*, meaning "driven on"

im•pul•sive
(im-**puhl**-siv)

adjective   acting without thinking about the possible results or dangers. *The impulsive behavior of my brother made my parents worry.*

Origin: Latin *impulsivus*, meaning "driven onwards"

in•cen•tive
(in-**sen**-tiv)

noun   something that encourages you to do something. *As an incentive to study, my mother promised to take me to the movies if I got a good grade on my test.*

in•ci•dence
(**in**-suh-duhns)

noun   the number of times something unpleasant happens. *An increased police presence has reduced the incidence of shoplifting in town.*

Origin: Latin *incidere*, meaning "fall upon," "happen to"

in•cli•na•tion
(in-kluh-**nay**-shuhn)

noun   a feeling that makes you want to do something. *Since I love fish, my inclination is to go to the new seafood restaurant.*

Origin: Latin *inclinare*, meaning "bend towards"

in•clined
(in-**klinde**)

adjective   likely to do something or act a certain way. *After taking the same route for a year, the driver was less inclined to try a new, unfamiliar route.*

Origin: Latin *inclinare*, meaning "bend towards"

in•come
(**in**-kuhm)

noun   money that a person earns from a job or other source. *Those with college degrees often have higher incomes than those without.*

in•con•ven•ience
(in-kuhn-**vee**-nyuhns)

noun   problems caused by someone or something which affect or annoy you. *The power outage was an inconvenience because I had to do my homework by candlelight.*

Origin: Latin *inconvenientia*, meaning "incongruity, inconsistency"

in•con•ven•ienced
(in-kuhn-**veen**-yuhnsd)

verb   affected or annoyed by problems caused by someone or something else. *The morning traffic inconvenienced many people on their way to work.*

Origin: Latin *inconvenientia*, meaning "incongruity, inconsistency"

in•cur
(in-**kur**)

verb   to have to pay money or another debt because of something you bought or had to pay for. *Some students incur a large debt to pay for college tuition.*

Origin: Latin *incurrere*, meaning "to run into"

in•di•cate
(**in**-di-kate)

verb   to show or point out something. *Alicia's race time would indicate if she had run fast enough to qualify for the finals.*

Origin: Latin *indicat-*, meaning "pointed out"

in•di•ca•tion
(in-di-**kay**-shuhn)

noun   a sign or piece of information that points something out. *The morning temperature was a good indication that it would be a warm day.*

Origin: Latin *indicat-*, meaning "pointed out"

in•di•vid•u•al•ized
(in-duh-**vij**-oo-al-ized)

adjective   made to fit the special needs of a certain person or thing. *The tutor came up with an individualized study plan for each student.*

Origin: Latin *individualis*, meaning "not divisible"

in•ex•pe•ri•enced
(in-ik-**spihr**-ee-uhnst)

adjective   not having skills or knowledge because you have never done something or have not done something for a long time. *Since Sam was an inexperienced cook, he decided to take a class at the community college to learn more.*

Origin: Latin *inexperientia*, meaning "no experience"

ACADEMIC GLOSSARY

in•i•tia•tive
(i-**nish**-uh-tiv)

noun an important new plan or process that has been started in order to solve a particular problem. *The candidate outlined several new initiatives she would put in place if she were elected.*

Origin: Latin *initiare*, meaning "beginning"

in•no•vate
(in-uh-**vayt**)

verb to introduce new ideas or methods of doing something. *In order to stay successful, companies must constantly innovate and create new products to sell.*

Origin: Latin *innovatus*, meaning "to change"

in•no•va•tion
(in-uh-**vay**-shuhn)

noun the introduction of new ideas or methods. *Because nobody had ever seen anything like it, the company's new product was called a major innovation.*

Origin: Latin *innovatus*, meaning "to change"

in•stance
(**in**-stuhns)

noun an example of a particular type of situation. *The principal knows of one instance when a student cheated on a test.*

Origin: Latin *instantia*, meaning "presence"

in•sti•tu•tion
(in-stuh-**too**-shuhn)

noun a large organization/group that has a certain kind of work or purpose, especially of a public nature. *Our town has enough banks and doesn't need another financial institution.*

Origin: Latin *instituo*, meaning "build or establish"

in•tend
(in-**tend**)

verb to plan to do something. *The group intends to study in the library after school.*

Origin: Latin *intendere*, meaning "direct, aim at"

in•ter•act
(in-tur-**akt**)

verb to act in a way that has an effect on someone. *Raising your hand and waiting to be called on is an appropriate way to interact with your teacher during class.*

in•ter•ac•tive
(in-tur-**ak**-tiv)

adjective when you can communicate with a computer system or program and have it react to your actions. *The school purchased new computers so that students could use them for interactive lessons.*

in•ter•est
(**in**-trist)

noun the extra money paid for borrowing money. *Interest is added to a credit card bill if it has not been fully paid.*

Origin: Latin *interesse*, meaning "make a difference"

in•ter•vene
(in-tur-**veen**)

verb to get involved in a difficult situation. *The parents decided to intervene when the children couldn't solve the argument on their own.*

Origin: Latin *intervenire*, meaning "to come between"

in•ter•ven•tion
(in-tur-**ven**-shuhn)

noun an action taken to change a difficult situation. *The problem was out of control and required an immediate intervention to put an end to it.*

Origin: Latin *intervenire*, meaning "to come between"

in•var•i•a•ble
(in-**var**-ee-uh-buhl)

adjective never changing. *The order of the months in a year are invariable.*

Origin: Latin *invariabilis*, meaning "not diverse"

in•var•i•a•bly
(in-**var**-ee-uh-blee)

adverb in every case; always. *Invariably, we have a surprise test every time I don't study the night before.*

Origin: Latin *invariabilis*, meaning "not diverse"

in•vest
(in-**vest**)

verb to spend money by buying something that you believe will give you a successful result in the future. *The speaker told students to invest in their education, because it would pay off later.*

Origin: Latin *investire*, meaning "to clothe, surround"

in•vest•ment
(in-**vest**-ment)

noun something you buy or do that will be useful later. *Adding money to your savings account is a good investment, as you might need that money later on.*

Origin: Latin *investire*, meaning "to clothe, surround"

in•volve
(in-**vahlv**)

verb to be a part of an activity or situation; to include something. *My mom tries to involve my brother and me when planning a family event.*

Origin: Latin *involvere*, meaning "to roll up, envelop"

li•a•bil•i•ty
(lye-uh-**bil**-i-tee)

noun something that is likely to cause problems for someone. *Staying up the night before an important test may be a liability later on.*

lin•guis•tic
(ling-**gwis**-tik)

adjective relating to language and words. *My lack of linguistic ability makes it hard for me to learn other languages.*

Origin: Latin *lingua*, meaning "language"

ACADEMIC GLOSSARY

man•date
(**man**-date)
1. *verb* to officially require something to be done. *My mom has begun to mandate that my sister and I do our own laundry.*
2. *noun* an official order to do something. *Our town needs a mandate that forbids people from parking by street corners.*
Origin: Latin *mandatum,* meaning "something commanded"

ma•ture
(muh-**choor** or muh-**toor**)
adjective fully grown or developed; to act older than your age. *The puppy grew into a mature dog within a year.*
Origin: Latin *maturus,* meaning "ripe"

men•tor
(**men**-tore or **men**-tur)
noun someone who helps another person with less knowledge or experience. *A guidance counselor can be a great mentor for students.*
Origin: Greek *Mentōr,* the name of an advisor from Homer's *Odyssey*

me•tab•o•lism
(muh-**tab**-uh-liz-uhm)
noun the process in the body that changes food into energy for working and growing body and mind. *Eating breakfast helps your metabolism and gives you energy.*
Origin: Greek *metabolē,* meaning "change"

mind•set
(**minde**-set)
noun someone's way of thinking about things, which is often difficult to change. *It is always difficult to change my parents' mindset when it comes to my curfew.*

min•i•mize
(**min**-uh-mize)
verb to reduce something as much as possible. *The school calendar helps minimize any confusion about which days students have off.*

min•i•mum
(**min**-uh-muhm)
1. *noun* the smallest amount allowed or needed. *A basketball team requires a minimum of five players, but the coach would prefer to have seven or eight.*
2. *adjective* describing the smallest amount allowed or needed. *Schools require students to attend a minimum number of days each year.*
Origin: Greek *minimus,* meaning "least"

mon•o•lin•gual
(mah-nuh-**ling**-gwuhl)
adjective speaking only one language. *Any monolingual students must take classes to learn a second language.*
Origin: Greek *mono,* meaning "single," + Latin *lingua,* meaning "tongue, language"

net•works
(**net**-wurks)
1. *noun* groups of people or organizations that communicate with each other and can help each other. *The Internet helps people in different professional networks connect with each other.*
2. *verb* meets other people who do the same type of work in order to share information or help each other. *My teacher networks with teachers in other schools to share ideas and lesson plans.*

non•vi•o•lence
(non-**vye**-uh-luhns)

noun　the use of peaceful means to bring about political or social change. *The protestors used nonviolence to peacefully relay their message.*

Origin: Latin *non*, meaning "not," + *violentia*, meaning "vehement, violent"

no•tion
(**noh**-shun)

noun　an idea or belief. *Where did you get the notion that we have early dismissal tomorrow?*

Origin: Latin *notio*, meaning "idea"

nov•ice
(**nah**-vis)

noun　someone who is just beginning to learn a skill or activity. *A novice needs a lot of support from more experienced people.*

Origin: Latin *novicius*, meaning "new"

ob•li•ga•tion
(ahb-li-**gay**-shuhn)

noun　something you have to do because it is your responsibility or because you have promised. *Stephi had an obligation to go to her brother's baseball game, since he attended her band concert.*

Origin: Latin *obligatio*, meaning "to bind"

ob•sta•cles
(**ob**-stuh-kuhls)

noun　things that make it difficult to do something. *Helen Keller inspired others because she overcame difficult obstacles.*

Origin: Latin *obstaculum*, meaning "obstruction"

ob•vi•ous
(**ahb**-vee-uhs)

adjective　clear or easy to notice or understand. *Once Angel understood how to solve the problem, the answer was obvious.*

Origin: Latin *obvius*, meaning "exposed"

or•gan•ize
(**or**-guh-nize)

verb　to prepare for and manage an event or an activity. *I volunteered to help organize our school carnival.*

Origin: Latin *organizare*, meaning "instrument, tool"

or•gan•iz•ers
(**or**-guh-ni-zers)

noun　people who prepare for and manage an event or activity. *The organizers of the event felt that their ideas helped make it a success.*

Origin: Latin *organizare*, meaning "instrument, tool"

pas•sive
(**pass**-iv)

adjective　tending to accept conditions; not taking action. *The student decided to take a passive approach and not confront the problem.*

Origin: Latin *passivus*, meaning "suffered"

pe•ri•od•i•cal•ly
(peer-ee-**ah**-dik-al-lee)

adverb　at regular times. *The magazine is released periodically, so a new issue is printed every month.*

ACADEMIC GLOSSARY

per•se•ver•ance
(pur-suh-**veer**-uhns)
noun   continuing to try doing something, even if it is difficult. *Eli was behind for most of the race, but his perseverance helped him get third place in the marathon.*
Origin: Latin *perseverer*, meaning "continue"

per•se•vere
(pur-suh-**veer**)
verb   to continue trying to do something, even if it is difficult. *Recovering from the accident helped me learn that I can get through anything if I persevere.*
Origin: Latin *perseverer*, meaning "continue"

per•sist
(pur-**sist**)
verb   to keep on doing something difficult. *If you persist in singing loudly, I'm going to study in another room.*
Origin: Latin *persistere*, meaning "stand firm"

per•sis•tence
(pur-**sis**-tuhns)
noun   the determination to keep on doing something difficult. *My persistence paid off when my dad finally agreed to let me go to the movie I had been asking to see.*
Origin: Latin *persistere*, meaning "stand firm"

pol•i•cy
(**pol**-uh-see)
noun   a rule or official way of doing something. *A common school policy is no running in the hallways.*
Origin: Greek *politeia*, meaning "citizenship"

po•ten•tial
(puh-**ten**-shuhl)
1. *adjective*   possible, but not yet actual or real. *The storm poses a potential threat to the entire east coast.*
2. *noun*   the possibility that something will develop in a certain way. *The potential for bad weather meant that our school's field day would likely be canceled.*
Origin: Latin *potentialis*, meaning "power"

po•ten•tial•ly
(puh-**ten**-shuhl-lee)
adverb   having the possibility of developing in a certain way. *It looked like it could potentially rain, so I made sure to bring an umbrella with me on my walk.*
Origin: Latin *potentialis*, meaning "power"

pre•cede
(pree-**seed**)
verb   to come before something else. *Tomorrow will begin with an assembly, which will precede your classes for the day.*
Origin: Latin *praecedere*, meaning "to go before"

pre•cise
(pri-**sise**)
adjective   very accurate or exact. *The gymnast takes precise steps so he will not fall.*
Origin: Latin *praecisus*, meaning "cut short"

pre•dic•tive
(pri-**dikt**-iv)

adjective   having to do with the ability to show what will happen in the future. *The boring start to the movie was predictive, since it did not get more interesting.*

Origin: Latin *praedicere*, meaning "warn, foretell"

pre•dic•tor
(pri-**dikt**-tur)

noun   something that shows what will happen in the future. *The dark clouds were a good predictor that it was about to rain.*

Origin: Latin *praedicere*, meaning "warn, foretell"

prep•a•ra•tion
(prep-uh-**ray**-shuhn)

noun   the process of making someone or something ready. *The preparation for the band's national tour included many weeks of rehearsal.*

Origin: Latin *praeparare*, meaning "make ready"

prepare
(pri-**pair**)

verb   to get ready; to help make someone or something ready. *In order to prepare for each game, the players practiced every day after school.*

Origin: Latin *praeparare*, meaning "make ready"

pri•mar•y lan•guage
(**prye**-mair-ee or **prye**-muh-ree **lang**-gwij)

noun   the language that someone uses most often. *The primary language spoken in the U.S. is English.*

Origin: Latin *primus*, meaning "first," + *lingua*, meaning "tongue, language"

prin•ci•ple
(**prin**-suh-puhl)

noun   a basic rule or idea. *A common principle is to treat others the way you would like to be treated.*

Origin: Latin *principium*, meaning "source"

pri•or•i•ty
(prye-**or**-uh-tee)

noun   something that is more important than other things. *My grades are my priority, so I always make sure my homework is finished before I do anything else.*

Origin: Latin *prior*, meaning "in front"

proc•ess
(**prah**-ses or **proh**-ses)

noun   a series of things that happen naturally and result in gradual change. *The process of learning a language can be a challenging, but also a rewarding, experience.*

Origin: Latin *porcessus*, meaning "progression, course"

proc•ess•ed
(**prah**-sesst)

1. *verb*   to have dealt with something in an official way. *The scorekeeper processed the results of the tournament and declared our team the winner.*

2. adjective   relating to foods that have substances added to them before they are sold that give them color or keep them fresh. *Processed cheese lasts longer than cheese that is not processed because of its added ingredients.*

Origin: Latin *processus*, meaning "progression, course"

pro•duc•tive
(pruh-**duhk**-tiv)

adjective   achieving a lot. *I knew I had to be productive during study hall because I would not have time to do my homework after school.*

Origin: Latin *productivus*, meaning "brought forth"

pro•fes•sion•al
(pruh-**fesh**-uh-nuhl)

noun   someone who works in a job that requires special education or training. *An internship at a newspaper is useful preparation for a student who would like to be a professional.*

pro•found
(pruh-**found**)

adjective   important and having a strong influence or effect. *The family felt profound joy when they saw their home was not damaged by the flood.*

Origin: Latin *profundus*, meaning "deep"

pro•hib•it
(proh-**hib**-it)

verb   to officially say that an action is illegal or not allowed. *Most restaurants prohibit customers from smoking because the smoke may bother others.*

Origin: Latin *prohibere*, meaning "prevent"

pro•long•ed
(pruh-**lawngd**)

adjective   continuing for a long time. *The prolonged power outage has left the community without electricity for two weeks.*

Origin: Latin *prolongare*, meaning "lengthen"

pro•mote
(pruh-**mote**)

verb   to help something grow or become more successful or well known. *The campaign was started to help promote healthy eating in the community.*

Origin: Latin *promovere*, meaning "move forward"

pro•mo•tion
(pruh-**moh**-shuhn)

noun   an activity to help something grow or become more successful or well known. *The band's concert tour was a promotion for their new album.*

Origin: Latin *promovere*, meaning "move forward"

pro•po•nents
(pruh-**poh**-nuhnts)

noun   people who support something. *The proponents of the law would like to see it passed and put into effect.*

Origin: Latin *proponere*, meaning "put forward"

pro•posed
(pruh-**pozed**)

verb   to have formally suggested a plan or an idea. *Residents of the neighborhood were excited to see drawings of what the planner proposed for the park.*

Origin: Latin *proponere,* meaning "put forward"

pro•spec•tive
(pruh-**spek**-tiv)

adjective   likely to do a particular thing or achieve a particular position. *A college admissions counselor is here to interview prospective students.*

pro•voke
(pruh-**voke**)

verb   to make someone very angry, especially by annoying them. *The students provoke their teacher by continually texting during class.*

pu•ber•ty
(**pyoo**-bur-tee)

noun   the time when a person's body changes from a child to an adult. *Puberty commonly occurs in young adolescents.*

Origin: Latin *pubertas,* meaning "adult"

re•al•i•ty
(ree-**al**-i-tee)

noun   what actually happens or is true, not what is imagined or thought. *Ali enjoys reading nonfiction books because they are about what happens in reality.*

Origin: Latin *realis,* meaning "real"

reg•is•ter
(**rej**-i-stur)

verb   to enter your name on an official list. *You must complete this form with your name and address if you want to register to vote.*

Origin: Latin *regestrum,* meaning "things recorded"

reg•is•tered
(**rej**-uh-sturd)

adjective   entered or recorded on an official list. *A United States citizen must be registered in order to vote in a presidential election.*

Origin: Latin *regestrum,* meaning "things recorded"

reg•u•late
(**reg**-yuh-late)

verb   to manage or control, especially by rules. *The principal must regulate a school by enforcing the rules.*

Origin: Latin *regula,* meaning "rule"

rel•e•vance
(**rel**-uh-vuhns)

noun   relating to an issue or a matter. *Because our tastes are so different, my parents' interests have no relevance to my own at all.*

Origin: Latin *relevare,* meaning "raise, lighten"

rel•e•vant
(**rel**-uh-vuhnt)

adjective   directly relating to an issue or a matter. *Your question is relevant because it is about what we are discussing in class.*

Origin: Latin *relevare,* meaning "raise, lighten"

ACADEMIC GLOSSARY

re•luc•tant
(ri-**luhk**-tuhnt)
adjective   not wanting to do something.
Abi was reluctant to cut her hair short since she was not sure if she would like it.
Origin: Latin *reluctari*, meaning "struggle against"

re•luc•tant•ly
(ri-**luhk**-tuhnt-lee)
adverb   in a slow or unwilling way.
Claiming that it was her least favorite chore, Marisa reluctantly took out the trash.
Origin: Latin *reluctari*, meaning "struggle against"

re•me•di•al
(ri-**mee**-dee-uhl)
adjective   meant to help or correct, often for students who have difficulty learning something. *Remedial classes helped me increase my ability to comprehend what I read.*
Origin: Latin *remedialis*, meaning "cure, medicine"

rep•re•sen•ta•tive
(rep-ri-**zen**-tuh-tiv)
adjective   describing a system of government made up of people who act and speak for the people who voted for them. *Congress is a representative body because they are elected by United States citizens.*
Origin: Latin *repraesentare*, meaning "to present"

re•quire
(ri-**kwire**)
verb   to demand something by law or rule.
Next year, the gym teacher will require us to wear uniforms in his class.
Origin: Latin *requirere*, meaning "need"

re•quire•ment
(ri-**kwire**-muhnt)
noun   something that must be done by law or rule. *I'm thankful that it is not a requirement to attend school on Saturday.*
Origin: Latin *requirere*, meaning "need"

re•sil•ience/re•sil•iency
(ri-**zil**-yuhnss/ri-**zil**-yuhn-see)
noun   the ability to return to normal after a difficult situation or event. *The resilience of the team members helped them stay positive after losing the big game.*

re•sis•tance
(ri-**zis**-tuhns)
noun   a refusal to accept new ideas or changes. *An attempt to lengthen the school day has been met with resistance from the community, who opposes the plan.*
Origin: Latin *resistentia*, meaning "hold back"

res•o•lu•tion
(rez-uh-**loo**-shuhn)
noun   an agreed-upon solution to a problem. *My sister and I are not allowed out of the house until we come to a resolution that ends our disagreement.*
Origin: Latin *resolvere*, meaning "loosen, release"

re•solve
(ri-**zahlv**)

verb to find a solution to a problem or to settle a difficulty. *I would like to see countries resolve their differences and end their conflicts with each other.*

Origin: Latin *resolvere*, meaning "loosen, release"

re•spond
(ri-**spahnd**)

verb to react to something that has been said or done. *It's hard, but the best way to respond to a bully is just to walk away.*

Origin: Latin *respondere*, meaning "answer"

re•sponse
(ri-**spons**)

noun a reaction to something that has been said or done. *I got a positive response when I read my essay to the class.*

Origin: Latin *respondere*, meaning "answer"

re•spon•sive
(ri-**spon**-siv)

adjective reacting quickly and in a positive way. *Because it was a beautiful day, everyone was very responsive to the idea of holding class outside.*

Origin: Latin *respondere*, meaning "answer"

re•spon•sive•ness
(ri-**spon**-siv-ness)

noun the quality or state of reacting quickly and in a positive way. *The responsiveness of the patient gave the doctors hope that she would recover.*

Origin: Latin *respondere*, meaning "answer"

re•strict•ed
(ri-**strikt**-ed)

adjective limited or controlled. *A fence was built to keep the public out of restricted areas that only certain people have access to.*

Origin: Latin *restrict-*, meaning "confined, bound fast"

re•stric•tion
(ri-**strikt**-shuhn)

noun a rule or law that limits what you can do or what can happen. *To decrease texting during class, a restriction was placed on the use of cell phones during school.*

Origin: Latin *restrictus*, meaning "tie tight"

re•struc•ture
(ri-**strukt**-chur)

verb to change the way something is organized; to change the terms of debts. *The teacher restructured the job chart so that each student now had a different task to perform.*

re•tain
(ri-**tayn**)

verb to keep something or continue to have something; to remember. *After many hours of studying, the students hoped they would retain all that they had read.*

Origin: Latin *retinere*, meaning "to hold back"

re•ten•tion
(ri-**ten**-shuhn)

noun the ability to keep something in your memory. *Cameron's retention of dates means that he never forgets his friends' birthdays.*

Origin: Latin *retinere*, meaning "to hold back"

re•veal•ed
(ri-**veeld**)

verb   made known something that had been unknown. *The hip hop performer revealed a new dance step at the show.*

Origin: Latin *revelare*, meaning "uncover"

risk
(**risk**)

noun   the chance that something bad or dangerous may happen; something likely to cause harm or danger. *Missing my curfew is a risk I am not willing to take in order to see the band play tomorrow.*

risk of
(**risk uhv**)

noun   a phrase that describes the potential for something bad or dangerous to happen. *The risk of walking along the steep mountain trail was too great, so the hikers chose to turn around.*

role
(**rohl**)

noun   the way in which someone or something is involved in an activity or situation. *Eating numerous fruits and vegetables daily plays an important role in a healthy lifestyle.*

seg•re•ga•tion
(seg-ri-**gay**-shuhn)

noun   the act or practice of keeping people or groups apart. *After segregation became illegal, children of all races were able to attend school together.*

Origin: Latin *segregare*, meaning "separate from others"

se•man•tic
(se-**man**-tik)

adjective   relating to the meanings of words. *Why is understanding the semantic difference between the words "upset" and "devastated" important?*

Origin: Greek *sēmantikos*, meaning "to signify or represent something"

sig•nif•i•cant
(sig-**nif**-i-kuhnt)

adjective   large or important enough to have an effect on something. *The most significant person in my life is my grandmother, because she has taken care of me since I was a baby.*

Origin: Latin *significare*, meaning "to show by signs, signify"

sig•nif•i•cant•ly
(sig-**nif**-i-kuhnt-lee)

adverb   in an important or noticeable way. *The extra support I received from my teacher significantly improved my grade.*

Origin: Latin *significare*, meaning "to show by signs, signify"

si•mul•ta•ne•ous•ly
(sye-muhl-**tay**-nee-uhs-lee)

adverb   doing two things at the same time. *It is difficult to study while simultaneously listening to music and reading.*

Origin: Latin *simul*, meaning "at the same time"

sleep dep•ri•va•tion
(**sleep** dep-ri-**vay**-shuhn)

noun   a lack of sleep needed over time. *Because sleep deprivation can negatively affect concentration, it is important that teens get enough rest every night.*

Origin: Latin *privare*, meaning "to deprive"

sleep-de•prived
(**sleep** di-**prived**)

adjective   lacking the sleep needed over a period of time. *Jon had a sleep-deprived night because thunderstorms had kept him awake.*

Origin: Latin *privare*, meaning "to deprive"

spe•cial•i•za•tion
(spesh-ul-i-**za**-shuhn)

noun   the state of being focused on a particular thing or area. *The mechanic can fix many machines, but his specialization is rebuilding the engines of motorcycles.*

Origin: Latin *specialis*, meaning "individual, specific"

spe•cial•ty
(**spesh**-ul-tee)

noun   a person's particular skill or area of study. *After tasting her delicious cake, everyone agreed that the chef's specialty was dessert.*

Origin: Latin *specialis*, meaning "individual, specific"

stage
(**stayj**)

noun   a particular time or state that something reaches as it grows or develops. *My baby sister is at the stage where she is learning how to walk.*

Origin: Latin *stare*, meaning "to stand"

stam•i•na
(**stam**-uh-nuh)

noun   physical or mental strength that lets you continue doing something for a long time without getting tired. *I'm not sure I have the stamina to run a marathon, but I could manage a three-mile race.*

Origin: Latin *stamen*, meaning "thread spun by the Fates that represents the length of a person's life"

sta•tis•tic
(stuh-**tis**-tik)

noun   a number that represents a fact or measurement. *One statistic that researchers found troubling was the percentage of students who sleep less than four hours a night.*

sub•sti•tute
(**suhb**-stuh-toot)

1. *verb*   to use something new or different in place of something else. *The restaurant decided to substitute an apple for cookies in order to offer a healthier lunch.*

2. *noun*   something or someone new and different that you use in place of something or someone that had been used previously. *Our regular teacher is sick, so a substitute will administer the test.*

Origin: Latin *substitutus*, meaning "put in place of"

su•per•vised
(**soo**-pur-vized)

verb   to be in charge or make sure something is done correctly or safely. *Small children can go on the roller coaster as long as they are supervised by an adult who will make sure they stay safe.*

Origin: Latin *super*, meaning "over," + *videre*, meaning "see"

su•per•vi•sion
(soo-pur-**vi**-shuhn)

noun   the act of watching over an activity or person to make sure things are done safely or correctly. *The parents hired a babysitter so that their children would have adult supervision while they were out of the house.*

Origin: Latin *super*, meaning "over," + *videre*, meaning "see"

sup•ple•ment
(**suhp**-luh-muhnt)

1. *verb*   to add something to what you earn to increase it to an acceptable level. *Jaya works overtime at her job to supplement her income with the extra money.*

2. *noun*   something that you add to something else to make it complete. *The vitamin he takes daily is an important supplement to his diet because it provides extra vitamins.*

Origin: Latin *supplementum*, meaning "fill up, complete"

sur•vey
(**sur**-vay)

verb   to ask many people the same questions to find out their opinions. *I think we should survey the students to see which school improvement they feel is most needed.*

Origin: Latin *super*, meaning "over," + *videre*, meaning "see"

sus•cep•ti•ble
(suh-**sep**-ti-ble)

adjective   likely to have a particular illness or problem. *Running long distances without proper shoes makes student athletes more susceptible to injuries, such as shin splints.*

Origin: Latin *susceptibilis*, meaning "take up, sustain"

symp•tom
(**simp**-tuhm)

noun   something wrong with your body or mind that shows you are ill. *A temperature above 98.6 degrees is one symptom of a fever.*

Origin: Greek *symptōma*, meaning "symptom"

tech•ni•cal
(**tek**-nuh-kuhl)

adjective   of or having to do with science, engineering, mechanics, or making things work. *The concert couldn't start due to a technical problem with the lights.*

Origin: Greek *teknikos*, meaning "skillful"

tend to
(**tend too**)

verb   to be likely to act or think a certain way. *I tend to agree with my older brother because he and I have very similar ways of thinking.*

Origin: Latin *tendere*, meaning "to stretch"

ten•den•cy
(**ten**-duhn-see)

noun   part of your character that makes you likely to act or think a certain way. *The shy girl had a tendency to speak quietly.*

Origin: Latin *tendere*, meaning "to stretch"

trait
(**trayt**)

noun   a quality that makes someone or something different. *One of the captain's best traits is her ability to be a leader.*

Origin: Latin *tractus*, meaning "drawing, pulling"

trend
(**trend**)

noun a general direction in which things are changing. *Stores often bring in new products to keep up with whatever trend is popular.*

ul•ti•mate
(**uhl**-tuh-mit)

adjective final; happening at the end of a process. *The teacher's ultimate goal was to one day become a principal.*

Origin: Latin *ultimatus*, meaning "come to an end"

ul•ti•mate•ly
(**uhl**-tuh-mit-lee)

adverb finally; after everything has been done. *After a long discussion, it was ultimately decided that practice would end early.*

Origin: Latin *ultimatus*, meaning "come to an end"

un•au•tho•rized
(uhn-**aw**-thuh-rized)

adjective without official approval or permission. *The singer was not involved in writing that unauthorized biography of her life.*

Origin: Latin *auctor*, meaning "author"

un•su•per•vised
(uhn-**soo**-per-vized)

adjective not watched over to make sure something or someone is safe or correct. *The teens were told that they were not allowed to be in the store unsupervised and that they needed to find an adult to accompany them.*

Origin: Latin *super*, meaning "over," + *videre*, meaning "see"

val•u•a•ble
(**val**-yoo-uh-buhl or **val**-yuh-buhl)

adjective of great use. *I hope to be a more valuable part of the team next year, since many of our best players are graduating.*

Origin: Latin *valere*, meaning "be strong"

val•ued
(**val**-yood)

adjective having a certain worth. *It turns out that the old picture I found in our attic is valued at several hundred dollars.*

Origin: Latin *valere*, meaning "be strong"

vi•o•late
(**vye**-uh-late)

verb to break or ignore a promise, rule, or law. *People who choose to violate the speed limit and drive too fast often get a ticket.*

Origin: Latin *violare*, meaning "treat violently"

vi•o•la•tion
(vye-uh-**la**-shuhn)

noun an action that breaks or ignores a promise, rule, or law. *It is considered a violation of the law to take something without paying for it.*

Origin: Latin *violare*, meaning "treat violently"

virtual
(**vur**-choo-uhl)

adjective made, done, or seen on a computer rather than in the real world. *Virtual money may one day replace paper dollars and coins.*

Origin: Latin *virtualis*, meaning "virtue"

Issue 1: Teen Sleep

Grady, D. (2002, November 5). Sleep is one thing missing in busy teenage lives. *The New York Times*, p. F5.

Maas, J. B. & Robbins, R. S. (2010). Sleep for success. In *Archives of ask a scientist*. Retrieved from http://www.ccmr.cornell.edu/education/ask/?quid=25

National Institute of Neurological Disorders and Stroke. (2007). Sleep: A dynamic activity. In *Brain basics: Understanding sleep*. Retrieved from http://www.ninds. nih.gov/disorders/brain_basics/understanding_sleep.htm

National Sleep Foundation. (2006). Summary findings of the 2006 Sleep in America poll. In *2006 teens and sleep*. Retrieved from http://www.sleepfoundation.org/ sites/default/files/2006_summary_of_findings.pdf

National Sleep Foundation. (2011). 2011 Summary of findings. In *2011 technology use and sleep*. Retrieved from http://www.sleepfoundation.org/sites/default/files/ sleepinamericapoll/SIAP_2011_Summary_of_Findings.pdf

Participatory Politics Foundation. (2009). H.Con.Res.176 - Zzz's to A's resolution. Retrieved from http://www.opencongress.org/bill/111-hc176/show

Shellenbarger, S. (2012, October 16). Understanding the zombie teen's body clock. *The Wall Street Journal*.

Weir, K. (2005, October). Who needs sleep? *Current Health 2, 32*(2), 16–19.

Issue 2: Learning Languages

Damschen, K. (2012, February 9). Many benefits come with learning a foreign language. *Standard Examiner*.

Language. (2013). In *Encyclopædia Britannica*. Retrieved from http://www.britannica. com/EBchecked/topic/329791/language

Espaillat, R. P. (1998). Bilingual/Bilingüe. In *Where horizons go* (p. 60). Kirksville, MO: New Odyssey Press.

Lusin, N. (2012, March). *The MLA survey of postsecondary entrance and degree requirements for languages other than English, 2009–10*. Retrieved from Modern Language Association Web site: http://www.mla.org/pdf/requirements_ survey_200910.pdf

National Council of State Supervisors for Languages. (2010, March). *States with or considering high school foreign language graduation requirements*. Retrieved from http://www.ncssfl.org/docs/States%20with%20Foreign%20Language%20 Graduation%20Requirements%20-%20%20Revised%202010.pdf

Pinantoan, A. (2012, July 21). The effects of a second language on the brain. Retrieved from http://www.cerebralhacks.com/brain-exercises/the-effect-of-a-second-language-on-the-brain

Rhodes, N. C., & Pufahl, I. (2009, November). *Foreign language teaching in U.S. schools: Results of a national survey.* Retrieved from Center for Applied Linguistics Web site: http://www.cal.org/projects/executive-summary-08-09-10.pdf

Tyler, J. (2010, June 25). CIA unusually public over need for Arabic, Farsi speakers. American Public Media. Retrieved from http://www.marketplace.org

Issue 3: Teens Behind the Wheel

Centers for Disease Control and Prevention. (2012). Teen Drivers: Fact sheet. Retrieved from http://www.cdc.gov/Motorvehiclesafety/Teen_Drivers/teendrivers_factsheet.html

Davis, R. (2005, March 2). Is 16 too young to drive a car? *USA Today.*

Distraction.gov. (2013). Key facts and statistics. Retrieved from http://www.distraction.gov/content/get-the-facts/facts-and-statistics.html

Distraction.gov. (2013). Take the pledge. Retrieved from http://www.distraction.gov/content/get-involved/take-the-pledge.html

Governors Highway Safety Association. (2013, May). Distracted driving laws. Retrieved from http://www.ghsa.org/html/stateinfo/laws/cellphone_laws.html

Governors Highway Safety Association. (2013, May). Graduated driver licensing (GDL) laws. Retrieved from http://www.ghsa.org/html/stateinfo/laws/license_laws.html

Insurance Institute for Highway Safety. (2011). Teenage motor vehicle crash deaths by gender, 1975–2011. In Trends. Retrieved from http://www.iihs.org/research/fatality.aspx?topicName=Teenagers&year=2011

Jackson, N. M. (2011, March). DN'T TXT N DRV. *Current Health Teens, 37*(7), 7–9.

National Highway Traffic Safety Administration. (2013, April). 2011 Young drivers traffic safety facts. In *2011 Data.* Retrieved from http://www-nrd.nhtsa.dot.gov/Pubs/811744.pdf

Thompson, P. (2004, May). Imaging study shows brain maturing. Retrieved from the National Institute of Mental Health website: http://www.nimh.nih.gov/news/science-news/2004/imaging-study-shows-brain-maturing.shtml

Zernike, K. (2012, October 8). Unsafe behind the wheel? *The New York Times Upfront, 145*(3), 6–7.

Issue 4: Teens & Money

Charles Schwab & Co. (2011). *Charles Schwab 2011 teens and money survey findings: Insights into money attitudes, behaviors, and expectations of 16- to 18-year-olds.* Retrieved from http://www.aboutschwab.com/images/press/teensmoneyfactsheet.pdf

Chen, T. (2013). American household credit card debt statistics through 2012. Message posted to http://www.nerdwallet.com/blog/credit-card-data/average-credit-card-debt-household/

Federal Deposit Insurance Corporation. (2005, Spring). *If at first you don't succeed.* In *FDIC Consumer News.* Retrieved from http://www.fdic.gov/consumers/consumer/news/cnspr05/spring_05_color.pdf

Federal Deposit Insurance Corporation. (2006, Summer). *Start smart: Money management for teens: How to save, spend, and protect your cash.* In *FDIC Consumer News.* Retrieved from http://www.fdic.gov/consumers/consumer/news/cnsum06/sum_06_color.pdf

Federal Reserve. (2010, January). *What you need to know: New credit card rules.* Retrieved from http://www.federalreserve.gov/consumerinfo/files/wyntk_ccrules.pdf

Mandell, L. (2008). *The financial literacy of young American adults: Results of the 2008 national Jump$tart Coalition survey of high school seniors and college students.* Retrieved from http://www.jumpstart.org/assets/files/2008SurveyBook.pdf

Smillie, D. (2004, April 5). Bankrupt by 25. *The New York Times Upfront, 136*(12), 16–17.

Stephens, B. (2006, April/May). Buyer, beware! *Career World, 34*(6), 14–16.

Issue 5: Online Learning

Birkenes, A. and Brown, D. (2011, December 5). Cyber students: Should students be required to take online courses? *Current Events, 111*(9), 7.

Cline, E. (2011). *Ready player one.* New York, NY: Broadway Paperbacks.

Evergreen Education Group. (2012). Growth of K–12 online learning. Retrieved from http://www.connectionsacademy.com/resources/infographics/k-12-online-school-growth.aspx

Evergreen Education Group. (2012). Number of states with statewide online learning options. In *International Association for K–12 Online Learning, Fast facts about online learning* (p. 2). Retrieved from http://www.inacol.org/cms/wp-content/uploads/2012/11/iNACOL_fastfacts_October_2012.pdf

Gabriel, T. (2011, April 5). More pupils are learning online, fueling debate on quality. *The New York Times*, p. A.1.

International Association for K–12 Online Learning. (2012). Typical cost categories for online schools. Retrieved from the Evergreen Education Group website: http://kpk12.com/cms/wp-content/uploads/Figure-6-typical-cost-categories-for-online-schools.png

International Association for K–12 Online Learning. (2013, February). *iNACOL's fast facts about online learning*. Retrieved from http://www.inacol.org/cms/wp-content/uploads/2013/04/iNACOL_FastFacts_Feb2013.pdf

International Association for K–12 Online Learning. (2012, October). *iNACOL's fast facts about online learning*. Retrieved from http://www.inacol.org/cms/wp-content/uploads/2012/11/iNACOL_fastfacts_October_2012.pdf

Keeping Pace with K–12 Online and Blended Learning. (2012). States with multi-district fully online schools. Retrieved from the Evergreen Education Group website: http://kpk12.com/cms/wp-content/uploads/Figure-6-typical-cost-categories-for-online-schools.png

Issue 6: Ready to Work

ACT, Inc. (2012). The condition of college and career readiness. Retrieved from http://media.act.org/documents/CCCR12-NationalReadinessRpt.pdf

Alliance for Excellent Education. (2011, May). *Saving now and saving later: How high school reform can reduce the nation's wasted remediation dollars*. Retrieved from http://www.all4ed.org/files/SavingNowSavingLaterRemediation.pdf

Hart Research Associates. (2011, August 18). *One year out: Findings from a national survey among members of the high school graduating class of 2010*. Retrieved from the College Board Web site: http://media.collegeboard.com/homeOrg/content/pdf/One_Year_Out_key_findings%20report_final.pdf

Klein, J. (2012, May 14). Learning that works. *Time*, *179*(19).

O'Donovan, B. (2010, February/March). Look to the future. *Career World*, *38*(5), 12–14.

OI Partners, Inc. (2012, May 15). How to receive retention rewards for top performance. Message posted to http://www.oipartners.net/news-detail/12-05-15/How_to_Receive_Retention_Rewards_for_Top_Performance.aspx

U.S. Department of Education. (2008). CTE delivery system and offerings: 2008. In *Career/technical education (CTE) statistics*. Retrieved from http://nces.ed.gov/surveys/ctes/tables/h01.asp

U.S. Department of Education. (2009). Student participation in CTE: 2009. In *Career/technical education (CTE) statistics*. Retrieved from http://nces.ed.gov/surveys/ctes/tables/h123.asp

Wagner, T. (2012, April 13). Educating the next Steve Jobs. *The Wall Street Journal*, p. C2.

Issue 7: Voting & Citizenship

Associated Press Election Research Group, George Mason University. (2012). Presidential election voter statistics. Retrieved from http://www.statisticbrain. com/presidential-election-voter-statistics/

Center for Information & Research on Civic Learning and Engagement. (2008). New census data confirm increase in youth voter turnout in 2008 election. Retrieved from http://www.civicyouth.org/new-census-data-confirm-increase-in-youth-voter-turnout-in-2008-election/

Corporation for National and Community Service. (2011). Political action. In *Volunteering and civic life in America: Millennials*. Retrieved from http://www. volunteeringinamerica.gov/special/Millennials/Customize

Corporation for National and Community Service. (2011). Volunteer rate (2002– 2011). In *Volunteering and civic engagement among millennials*. Retrieved from http://www.volunteeringinamerica.gov/special/Millennials

Corporation for National and Community Service. (2011). Where people volunteer. In *Volunteering and civic engagement among millennials*. Retrieved from http://www.volunteeringinamerica.gov/special/Millennials

Galston, W. (2011, November 5). Telling Americans to vote, or else. *The New York Times*, p. SR9.

Hamilton, L. H., (2003, September 21). What does it mean to be an American citizen? Presented at the Congressional Conference on Civic Education.

National Archives. (n.d.). The Constitution of the United States, Amendments 11– 27. Retrieved May 1, 2013, from http://www.archives.gov/exhibits/charters/ constitution_amendments_11-27.html

Wiles, D. (2010). *Countdown*. New York, NY: Scholastic.

Issue 8: Failure or Success?

Carney, J. (2010, November 2). The politics of the authoritarian marshmallow test. Message posted to http://www.cnbc.com/id/39967670

Dweck, C. (2013). Interview by Jocelyn K. Glei. Talent isn't fixed and other mindsets that lead to greatness. Retrieved from http://99u.com/articles/14379/talent-isnt-fixed-and-other-mindsets-that-lead-to-greatness

Hanford, E. (2012, August). Angela Duckworth and the research on "Grit." American RadioWorks. Retrived from http://americanradioworks.publicradio.org/features/tomorrows-college/grit/angela-duckworth-grit.html

Kayden, S. (2013, February 11). *The brave boys of Greensboro. Scholastic Scope*, 61(7), 16–21.

Are you a loser? (2012, April 2). *Scholastic Scope*, 60(11), 16–18.

Seligman, M. E. P. (2001, April). Building resilience. *Harvard Business Review*, 89(3), 100–106.

VIA Institute on Character. (2013, March 13). *You: Decoded: VIA Me! Report for John Smith*. Retrieved from http://www.viacharacter.org/www/Portals/0/VIA%20Youth%20Sample.pdf

CREDITS

ISSUE 1: TEEN SLEEP

ISSUE 2: LEARNING LANGUAGES

ISSUE 3: TEENS BEHIND THE WHEEL

ISSUE 4: TEENS & MONEY

ISSUE 5: ONLINE LEARNING

"Cyber Students" by Adele Birkenes and Dontaé Brown from *Current Events* magazine, December 5, 2011. Published by Scholastic Inc. All rights reserved.

"More Pupils Are Learning Online, Fueling Debate on Quality" by Trip Gabriel from *The New York Times*, April 5, 2011. Copyright © 2011 by The New York Times. Reprinted by permission of The New York Times.

From *Ready Player One* by Ernest Cline. Copyright © 2011 by Dark All Day, Inc. Reprinted by permission of Crown Publishers, a division of Random House, Inc. All rights reserved.

Excerpt from *"Ready Player One*: An Interview with Author Ernest Cline" by Rebecca Serle from the *Huffington Post* website, August 17, 2011. Copyright © 2011 by Rebecca Serle. Reprinted by permission of the author.

ISSUE 6: READY TO WORK

"Look to the Future" by Betsy O'Donovan from *Career World*, February/March 2010. Copyright © 2010 by Scholastic Inc. All rights reserved.

"Learning That Works" by Joe Klein from *Time* magazine, May 14, 2012. Copyright © 2012 by Time Inc. Reprinted by permission of Time Inc.

"Educating the Next Steve Jobs" by Tony Wagner from The Wall Street Journal online, April 13, 2012. Copyright © 2012 by The Wall Street Journal. Reprinted by permission of Dow Jones & Co., Inc.

ISSUE 7: VOTING & CITIZENSHIP

"Telling Americans to Vote, or Else" by William A. Galston from *The New York Times*, November 5, 2011. Copyright © 2011 by The New York Times. Reprinted by permission of The New York Times.

"What Does it Mean to be an American Citizen?" by The Honorable Lee H. Hamilton from the Center on Congress at Indiana University website, September 21, 2003. Copyright © by Lee H. Hamilton. Reprinted by permission of the author.

From *Countdown* by Deborah Wiles. Copyright © 2010 by Deborah Wiles. Published by Scholastic Press, an imprint of Scholastic Inc. Reprinted by permission of Scholastic Inc.

ISSUE 8: FAILURE OR SUCCESS?

"Talent Isn't Fixed and Other Mindsets That Lead to Greatness" interview is from www.99u.com, a website that provides insights on making ideas happen. Copyright © 99U. Reprinted by permission.

"Angela Duckworth and the Research on 'Grit'" by Emily Hanford from American Public Media's American RadioWorks®. Copyright © 2012 by American Public Media. Reprinted by permission.

The Brave Boys of Greensboro by Spencer Kayden from *Scholastic Scope* magazine, February 11, 2013. Copyright © 2013 by Spencer Kayden. All rights reserved.

CREDITS